Pete Seeger
vs.
The
Un-Americans

A Tale of the Blacklist

Pete Seeger
vs.
The
Un-Americans

A Tale of the Blacklist

EDWARD RENEHAN

2014

New Street Communications, LLC

Wickford, RI

newstreetcommunications.com

2014
New Street Communications, LLC
Wickford, Rhode Island
newstreetcommunications.com

To

the memory of

Aaron Swartz

CONTENTS

Pete Seeger, the folksinger ... lives not far from me near Beacon, NY, and is loved by many people, young and old, who have enjoyed his music. ... He has refused to take the Fifth Amendment because he felt that could be construed as an admission of guilt, and chose instead to invoke the freedoms of the First Amendment. His case is now in the higher courts.

Eleanor Roosevelt, "My Day," January 15th, 1962

Pete had been around for years. He'd been in the popular folk group The Weavers, but had been blacklisted during the McCarthy era and had a hard time, but he never stopped.

Bob Dylan, *Chronicles*

This little light of mine, I'm gonna let it shine.

Old Spiritual

CHAPTER ONE:
SEEGER'S SLAVE GANGS

Beacon, NY – August 1955

Lee Hays – Pete Seeger's singing and songwriting partner from the Weavers – called them "Seeger's slave gangs." On a typical weekend a dozen or so friends (and not infrequently a number of mere banjo- and guitar-picking acquaintances) camped in tents outside the Seegers' little cabin on the mountainside, or lay their sleeping bags on the floor inside, and helped Pete and Toshi slowly but surely create the little compound they'd eventually call home for more than sixty years.

Pete had built the one-room cabin almost by himself over the course of the summer of 1949, right after purchasing the 17 acres on which it sat for $100 an acre – much of this money borrowed. Most of the land was the completely uninhabitable steep side of a mountain, but with a two-acre ledge half way up upon which Pete built the home. The sparse cabin's only hint of luxury was a large picture window looking out to the west across the wide Hudson to Newburgh and the mountains beyond.

On this particular day, Seeger and his elves busily worked away on an outbuilding that was to serve as a barn/garage, but also include a small second-floor office where Pete could work at correspondence or practice his music away from the distractions of the household, which now included three children. It was a traditional barn-raising, with all four walls ready to be hoisted up into place.

The first of these was about to ascend when a nearly immaculate black sedan – its bottom dusty and muddy after bouncing up Seeger's rustic, unkempt dirt driveway – rolled slowly into the clearing. A stern-looking man in a business suit emerged. "Are you Pete Seeger?" he asked, evidently already knowing the answer. After Pete responded in the affirmative, the man handed him a subpoena to testify before the House of Representatives Select Committee on Un-American Activities in two weeks time. Then he turned abruptly without another word, and walked back to his car.

CHAPTER TWO:
DOUBLE-EDGED SWORD

Most swords have two edges, and cut both ways. This seems yet another argument for beating them into plowshares.

The House of Representatives Select Committee on Un-American Activities (HUAC) was not founded by a conservative but rather a liberal. It was Samuel Dickstein – a Democratic Representative from New York's Lower East Side – who in 1934 successfully called for the establishment of a "Special Committee on Un-American Activities" to look into the doings of the German-American Bund movement and its ties to National Socialism in Germany. Later on, in 1938, the Committee became the House *Select* Committee on Un-American Activities, and was subsequently (1945) made a permanent "standing" Committee.

As of 1938, when it came under the chairmanship of conservative Texas Democrat Martin Dies, the emphasis of the "Dies Committee" investigations shifted away from right-wing un-Americans to the left-wing variety. (Dies's 1940 book *The Trojan Horse in America* [New York: Dodd, Mead & Co.] is a classic of myopic, jingoistic, nationalistic paranoia.) As would soon be the case with Joe McCarthy on the Senate side of the Capitol building, Dies had the habit of spotting what he purported to be subversive elements under just about every rock and behind just about every tree.

It is typical, writes Garry Wills, that "when the Committee was finally [made into a Select Committee in 1938], it was the result of a compromise with those who wanted to investigate radicals and socialists as well as Fascists. Liberals in America have often elaborated an ideological test which the right wing applies more broadly and ferociously than the liberals originally intended. ... All later excesses arise from the first principle of ideological self-testing. If it is not enough to possess citizenship and obey the laws, if one must also subscribe to the propositions of Americanism, then we create two classes of citizens – those loyal and pure in doctrine, and those who without actually breaking any laws, are considered un-American, insufficient in their Americanism. These latter can be harassed, spied on, forced to register, deprived of governmental jobs and other kinds of work."

Of course, it makes a great deal of difference, as political fads come and go and political power shifts, exactly who gets to define the "propositions of Americanism." One might easily be considered a patriot in one decade and a fifth columnist in another. One's enunciated thoughts might be viewed as entirely wholesome and "American" under one regime of public sentiment, and thunderously subversive under another. (It was, we should remember, an assembly of wholly subversive, traitorous and "un-British" forefathers who signed the Declaration of Independence.)

Upon the initial 1934 inauguration of the Committee, Dickstein as vice-chairman under the inimitable but generally disinterested John McCormack (later Speaker of the House), led the charge of issuing subpoenas and personally questioning each and every witness. One after another, mostly-German citizens associated, or even just suspected of being associated, with organizations sympathetic to Nazism (or Fascism in general), were brought up before the Committee and subjected to Dickstein's often acerbic, condescending and nearly-always bullying form of examination. (In fact, in his dramatic rhetoric and penchant for undocumented, exaggerated innuendo and accusation, Dickstein pioneered the same style of political theater to later be perfected by McCarthy.) Dickstein found himself bounced from the Committee after it came under the leadership of Dies. As the *Guardian* has noted, he "looked on powerlessly in 1939 as US 'brownshirts' under the leadership of the 'American Fuhrer,' Fritz Kuhn, rallied in Madison Square Garden."

I have spoken of two-edged swords. To put a fine point on this, it is worth going into a bit more detail on Samuel Dickstein. As has been documented in such highly-respected books as Allen Weinstein's and Alexander Vassiliev's *The Haunted Wood: Soviet Espionage in America – The Stalin Era* (New York: Random House, 1998), for a period of at least three years the left-leaning Dickstein served as an operative on the payroll of the Soviet NKVD (precursor to the KGB) at a salary of $1,250.00 per month. His mission: to unsettle anti-Communist and pro-Fascist organizations in the United States, and at the same time report back any useful information unearthed by Committee investigators which otherwise did not come out in public hearings.

According to the *Boston Globe*: "Dickstein ran a lucrative trade in illegal visas for Soviet operatives before brashly offering to spy for the NKVD ... in return for cash." (Dickstein's NKVD handlers, deducing that his interest might be more commercial than ideological, gave him the code-name "Crook.") Whatever Dickstein's personal motives, it seems likely that the entire concept of the HUAC, the organization which not long after its birth trained it sights on American Communism writ both small and large and thereafter did not alter course, originated not in Washington, but Moscow.

CHAPTER THREE:
FELLOW TRAVELERS

By the standards of Whittaker Chambers, easily the most famous of American ex-Communists – (former spy, fire-breathing supporter of the Cold War, key witness against Alger Hiss, and a man bent on revealing any and all Communist agents in places of power or influence) – Pete Seeger did not qualify as a Communist. Chambers wrote disdainfully of the unserious "thousands who continually drift into the Communist Party and out again. The turnover is vast."

No, Chambers said, the only real Communists were those, like him, who had become so fanatically devoted to the party that they would sacrifice everything and anything – as Chambers once had – in order to serve unquestioningly the party's program for the higher-good, and who did so for years. The only genuine Communists were those "dedicated revolutionists whose primary allegiance [is] no longer to any country – nor to those factors which give a country its binding force: tradition, family, community, soil, religious faith." All the rest were mere tourists on summer vacation – people who, when they ended their casual flirtation, did so easily and without undue pain or angst.

For Chambers, however, as with other true devotees and functionaries, the final split with Communist philosophy and doctrine – when and if it came – had the force and weight of a religious conversion. Writing in the *Foreword* to his autobiography *Witness*, Chambers made clear that when he broke with the party he did so "slowly, reluctantly, in agony," as if leaving a spiritual home.

This distinction between real vs. flirtatious reds is probably what allowed Chambers to sign a petition in 1959 demanding that Paul Robeson, having been denied a passport solely because of his vocal criticism of American race policies and his support for anti-Colonial movements in Africa, have his right to travel restored. (Note: Chambers also advocated for his nemesis Alger Hiss on the same issue, denounced the Objectivist philosophy of Ayn Rand in the pages of Bill Buckley's conservative *National Review,* and loudly condemned the nuclear arms race – all of these being issues upon which he and many liberals shared complete agreement. Chambers as well denounced Joseph McCarthy, writing to Buckley: "For the right to tie itself in any way to Senator McCarthy is suicide . . . What did he really accomplish? I would say: very close to nothing but noise ...")

During the 1930s and 40s the Communist Party of America (CPA) was awash in tourists – Pete Seeger,Woody Guthrie, and others of their circle among them. The generic term for such types was "fellow traveler." The phrase (попутчик, *poputchik*; literally: "one who travels the same path") had first come in to use as a pejorative one within Soviet Russia, denoting a citizen who casually tagged

along with the revolution as he or she might with any
fashion of the day – a political tailgater, if you will – but
would never dirty his or her hands with the real blood-
and-guts, life-or-death struggle that was true insurgency.

*

Young Seeger was a second-generation fellow
traveler. His father, musicologist Charles Seeger (1886 –
1979), was an academic who graduated from Harvard, did
graduate work in Cologne, and then served as instructor of
music at the University of California, Berkeley, until being
fired because of his vocal opposition, as a pacifist, to U.S.
entry into what came to be known as World War I.
(Charles's brother, the poet Alan Seeger, died in that war
while fighting with the French Foreign Legion on July 4th,
1916, during the Battle of the Somme.)

Charles subsequently taught at Juilliard, at New
York's Institute of Musical Art, and at the New School for
Social Research. During the late thirties, he lived in
Washington and served as musical adviser to a branch of
what became the Farm Security Administration. Charles
also served in various functions for the WPA (including as
Administrator of the WPA's Federal Music Project) and the
Pan American Union, before going on to teach at UCLA
from 1957 to 1971. Charles's last UCLA post (1961-1971)
was as Research Professor at the university's Institute of
Ethnomusicology.

Throughout his life, Charles always veered to the left politically. During the early thirties, he was a member (and for a time, chairman) of the Composers' Collective of New York. This was "a coterie of professional musicians seeking to forge a relationship between music, society, politics and the economy," writes Charles's biographer, Ann Pescatello. A "radical group with informal ties to the Communist Party, the Collective was at first a special section of the Pierre Degeyter Club, named for the French composer who wrote the workers' anthem, *L'Internationale* (1871)." A chief aim of the Collective was to "develop guidelines for new workers' music – songs for the masses. Art was to be a weapon in the class struggle ... ." Publications of the group included such volumes as *The Red Song Book, The New Workers' Songbook* and *Songs of the People* – all practical volumes meant to help invigorate the union movement through music.

Members of the Collective included Charles's second wife and Peter's step-mother, composer Ruth Crawford Seeger, as well as composers Earl Robinson, Elie Seigmeister, Herbert Haufrecht, Hanns Eisler and Aaron Copland. "The links between the Collective and the Communist Party varied. Some members belonged to the party, but most, including Seeger, never formally joined," says Pescatello. Looking back from the perspective of the 1970s, Charles was obviously not happy with much of his political activity decades before. "There is no reason why you should not take me to task for some of the outrageous things I said and did during the early thirties," Charles told Pescatello. "I was in an overwrought state of mind as any sensitive person must have been at the goings-on during the Depression. ... It took me fifteen years to discover the nature of Stalin."

Charles sometimes brought Peter – by the early 1930s a boarding student at the posh Avon Old Farms prep school in Connecticut – along to meetings of the Collective, where the teenager met his first Communists. "It was quite different from the cartoons of a person with a beard and a bomb," Pete said many years later. "I found these were highly organized, highly intelligent, argumentative people." Peter quickly kindled to their utopian flame. At Harvard, where he started in the autumn of 1936, joining the Class of '40 (which also included John Kennedy and Donald Regan, future Reagan Administration Treasury Secretary and Chief of Staff), Peter became a regular sight distributing Socialist literature in front of Widener Library.

Like another Harvard radical – the journalist and revolutionary John Reed, who graduated in 1910 alongside Peter's uncle Alan and wound up buried in the Kremlin Wall – Peter socialized little and was unenthusiastic about most of his classes. Such things seemed trivial as opposed to saving the world. During the summer of 1937, a fellow counselor at a Socialist summer camp quit to join the Abraham Lincoln Brigade and fight for Loyalist Spain against Franco's fascists, as did one of Seeger's old friends from Avon.

Back at Harvard, Peter joined up with Arthur Kinoy
(destined to become a defense attorney who represented
clients ranging from the Rosenbergs to the Chicago Seven)
in founding the radical *Harvard Progressive*. He also joined
the Young Communist League (YCL) – more of a social
club for left wingers, hosting dances and picnics and sports
events, than an active political organization – and
successfully ran for the office of Secretary of the liberal
American Student Union (ASU). He in turn left this post at
the end of the spring semester, 1938, when he lost his
scholarship due to poor grades and dropped out of school.
All the while he plunked on the banjo and guitar, and
almost any other instrument that came his way. Like his
father, he believed music could and should be used to
advance progressive political agendas.

By the time he – along with Woody Guthrie, Lee Hays,
Millard Lampbell and others – founded the Almanac
Singers in 1940, Seeger had done a stint working for Alan
Lomax at the Library of Congress's Archive of American
Folk Song (where he soaked up songs like a sponge) and
traveled cross-country with Guthrie, singing everywhere
from churches to saloons and union halls. The Almanacs
had a fluid roster of personnel (including Cisco Houston,
Josh White and Sonny Terry) which changed frequently
from gig to gig. Pete (calling himself "Pete Bowers" in
order to inoculate his Federally-employed father from
political reprisals) and Lee most always held center-stage:
the nucleus of the group. The Almanacs' repertoire was

avowedly political. And like virtually all of the American left at that time, they adhered closely to the Communist Party line.

In May of 1940, the group issued an almost-immediately-obscure recording of anti-war material entitled *Songs for John Doe*, this during the days of the Molotov/Ribbentrop non-aggression pact when the Communist line was firmly against U.S. entry into the European war. Most of the songs protested FDR's peacetime draft. The record label was "Keynote," a tiny endeavor owned by Eric Bernay, who also owned a small record shop on West 44th Street. (Given the highly controversial nature of the material, Bernay made the decision to stamp the 78s as being issued by "Almanac Records." Bernay – a radical and former treasurer of the *New Masses* – also insisted the Almanacs finance the pressing. In the end, record-producer John Hammond, composer Earl Robinson and Bernay circulated a letter to various progressive organizations soliciting funds to support the project.)

Soon after the release of the recording, Harvard political science and government professor Carl Friedrich included a brief mention of the Almanacs and their set of 78s in a lengthy essay appearing in the June number of the *Atlantic Monthly*, "These recordings are distributed under the innocuous appeal: 'Sing Out for Peace.' Yet they are strictly subversive and illegal. ... The three records sell for one dollar and you are asked to 'play them in your home, play them in your union hall, take them back to your people.' Probably some of these songs fall under the criminal provisions of the Selective Service Act, and to that extent it is a matter for the Attorney-General. But you can never handle situations of this kind democratically by mere suppression. Unless civic groups and individuals will make a determined effort to counteract such appeals by equally effective methods, democratic morale will decline."

In his essay, entitled "The Poison in Our System," Friedrich also singled out *Life* Magazine (owned by the conservative Henry Luce) as an instrument of fifth column propaganda. Ironically, that very same month, Luce's own *Time* published a lengthy critical review of *John Doe*.

One story has it that when shown the record, FDR dryly observed to Archibald MacLeish that it was nothing to worry about: "Only lefties are going to hear it anyway." To a large degree, he was right. Yet, despite the barely-noticeable bad reception for the obscure *John Doe*, the Almanacs drew praise from some notable quarters. After a performance by "Pete Bowers," Lee Hays and several other group members at an early spring '41 meeting of the League of American Writers, Theodore Dreiser told Pete: "If there were six more teams like you, we could save America."

Professor Friedrich soon had cause to relax with regard to the Almanacs. Seeger and his colleagues abruptly changed course as soon as Hitler broke the non-aggression treaty and invaded Soviet Russia in June of '41. "Our whole politics," remembered Lee, "took a terrible shift from 'the Yanks ain't coming' to 'the Yanks ARE coming ...'" The Almanacs themselves recalled every copy of *John Doe* that they could lay their hands on – an easy task, since the lion's share remained unsold – and saw to the destruction of most of the inventory. The group wanted to get as far away from their peace songs as was possible.

The Almanacs' main goal, however, had little to do with international relations or questions of war and peace. They saw their main mission as using song to strengthen and build a militant American labor movement. To this end, they produced a record of old and new labor organizing songs entitled *Talking Union,* and embarked on a coast to coast tour of unions and union halls. Seeger recalled the highlight of the tour being a July '41 appearance for the San Francisco branch of the International Longshore and Warehouse Union. One song – "The Ballad of Harry Bridges," about that Union's founder whom the U.S. Government had repeatedly tried and failed to deport to his native Australia – proved particularly popular.

Amid the enthusiastic crowd who clapped and cheered for the Almanacs, unbeknownst to all, sat an FBI agent who in his subsequent report criticized not only the performers but also the audience who sang along "not from their own desire, but [who] were led into it through mass psychology and apathy toward the utter control of the meeting by Communist officers and members." It didn't help things any that a line in the Bridges song explicitly insulted the FBI. Neither did the fact that only a few months later, Seeger – at age 22 – took out formal membership in the CPA.

Back in New York, the group featured a reworking of "Round and Round, Old Joe Clark," now titled "Round and Round Hitler's Grave," in all their performances. The Almanacs' recording of pro-war material, titled *Dear Mr. President,* came out in February 1942, on the heels of Pearl Harbor. Just before release of the recording, Alan Lomax and other supporters urged the Almanacs to change their name, replacing their old "Almanac" brand with something different for the new record. It was feared the group's old anti-war songs would catch up with them at a time when these were best left forgotten. Largely because of Seeger's stern objection, however, the name-change did not happen.

At first, the Almanac Singers rode a great wave of enthusiastic acceptance for their new tunes. Post Pearl Harbor, the Communist line and the American agenda harmonized quite nicely. In January of '42, the Almanacs – in the persons of Woody, Pete, Bess Lomax Hawes (Alan's sister) and Sis Cunningham (an Oklahoma songstress, songwriter and organizer) – found themselves singing for a nationwide audience on the CBS radio program "We the People." Concurrently, an agent at the venerable William Morris Agency took them on as clients. Even the management of the elaborate and expensive Rainbow Room, at the top of Rockefeller Center, asked the group to audition and eventually offered them a booking (which Seeger, Guthrie and company wound up turning down on ideological principle).

While this went on, their agent at William Morris began a final round of negotiations with Decca for an exclusive recording contract. To cap it all off, on February 14th, within days of the release of *Dear Mr. President,* the group performed for more than twenty-nine million listeners on the inaugural edition of a new, prime-time, coast-to-coast Saturday night broadcast: "This is War."

Then, suddenly, the ghost of *John Doe* returned to haunt the singers who had refused to change their name. Three days after the nationwide broadcast, the *New York Post* ran with the headline "Peace Choir Changes Tune," while the *World-Telegram* announced "Singers on New Morale Show Also Warbled for Communists." The William Morris agent disappeared. The Decca offer evaporated. Bookings were canceled. It was an experience Seeger and the others would repeat more than once in the years ahead.

CHAPTER FOUR:
SENTIMENTALISTS

In the years to come, the public mind would come to conflate all Communists and all fellow travelers into one extreme caricature: the Communist of the underground cell, the spy (*ala* Alger Hiss and the Rosenbergs), the traitor receiving and acting upon sealed secret orders from Moscow, the dark propagandist furtively using a powerful position in American media to subvert the patriotism, morale, and morals of the American public. The popular image was one of deception, dishonor and bad faith. The Communist was amoral – a broken soul bent by a twisted ideology into a thing of savage destruction and malice.

That a vast network of clandestine Moscow-directed operatives was active in the United States throughout the 1930s and 1940s cannot be disputed. But neither can the fact that publicly-affiliated members of the "open" party had absolutely nothing to do with these secret activities, and in fact were thought by Communist officials to be generally useless when it came to advancing the goals of the party in any significant way. Such was the case with Seeger and other naive, idealistic youngsters (including struggling novelist Howard Fast, future author of *Spartacus*) who climbed aboard at about this time. Such recruits were not viewed by the party as true revolutionaries. Theirs was the benign and respectable public organization that throughout the 30s had been active in advancing the cause of trade unionism, fought for civil rights, and argued against discrimination in the workplace.

During the 1930s and early 1940s, the CPA operated on two levels: the dynamic, widely-accepted, legitimate political party respected as one of the most vibrant tools of American progressivism, and the subversive cabal linked darkly to one of the most vicious and repressive regimes the world has ever known. Members of the open party had no clue that the underground wing even existed.

Before being asked to move from the saccharine open party to its dark alter ego, the religiously devoted Whittaker Chambers (in his time the most robust of doctrinaire true believers) had to spend a long period as an unimportant and highly-visible editor at the *Daily Worker* – this because his superiors at first considered him "a sentimentalist … harmless, foolish [but] useful, for he gets out the paper." Only once he'd demonstrated and proved his blindly ferocious commitment to the international class struggle (*aka*, Moscow), as well as his willingness to unquestionably follow any orders whatsoever, did Chambers graduate to other things, whereas the likes of Seeger and Fast would always be viewed for exactly what they were – lightweights: starry eyed idealists whose very lack of cynicism was viewed by party insiders as a fatal flaw.

What drove the underground engine of the party was traitorous ambition and coldly calculated intrigue. (Writing of Chambers's entry into the party underground, with its many malignant agendas, biographer Sam Tanenhaus notes that Chambers "exalted in his new identity. He had abdicated his place in the 'dying world' and had discovered a meaningful niche in the world waiting to be born.") What drove the open party of Seeger and Fast was patriotism: a firm and wholly admirable desire to improve the lives of Americans and make more real the national ideals of equality and justice. The devotion of those involved in illicit party work was not to country, but to international revolution and the world-wide defeat of capitalism. The devotion of the sentimentalists was to country, their own country, the United States – whereas *country* meant nothing to the true ideologue. The vital difference was dissent as opposed to deceit.

*

The growing FBI dossiers on Seeger, Guthrie and their associates did nothing to keep Pete out of the Army or Guthrie out of the Merchant Marine once war was finally declared. Others of the Almanacs scattered to various military and civilian fronts. The idea of fostering a singing labor movement went into hibernation. It was not until December of 1945 that Seeger – after having served several years as a private in the Army's Special Services Division

(variously at a number of stateside assignments and finally
in Saipan) – spearheaded the founding of People's Songs,
Inc. The goal, he explained years later, was to: "Make a
singing labor movement. Period. … I was hoping to have
hundreds, thousands, tens of thousands of union choruses.
Just as every church has a choir, why not every union."
The board included many Almanac alumni, not the least
Guthrie. Pete served as president, Lee Hays as executive-
secretary.

Now married to the brilliant and beautiful Toshi Ohta
– who was just as radical as she was smart, and also
something of an organizational genius – Pete worked
diligently on the new initiative. By the end of February
1946, People's Songs could boast affiliates in twenty states
and more than one thousand members. They started a
publication, the *People's Songs Bulletin*, which featured new
songs submitted by members nationwide. (It was during a
relatively boring meeting of the People's Songs board that
Lee and Pete wrote what would become a classic – "If I
Had a Hammer" [initially titled "The Hammer Song"] –
passing manuscript notes between them as the lyrics
slowly came into shape.) The organization even started a
folkish booking agency – People's Artists – and advertised
an impressive Board of Sponsors: Leonard Bernstein,
Aaron Copland, Lena Horne, Lincoln Kirstein, Judy
Holiday, John Houseman, Paul Robeson, Dorothy Parker
and Oscar Hammerstein II.

Amid all this, Seeger vainly sought help and cooperation from the CPA. But the organization was generally unresponsive, providing only rhetorical support. Lenin had once said "the revolution does not need historians." Neither, apparently, did it need folksingers. Per Seeger biographer David King Dunaway: "Because of his independence ... Seeger had a reputation [in the party] as an 'unreliable'; at least one Committee on 'backsliders' chided him for not having the right attitude." Irwin Silber – a party stalwart who would eventually come to manage the People's Songs office and later be involved with *Sing Out!* Magazine – complained more than once that Seeger's "basis in Marxism was [too] sketchy" to make him in any way an effective party functionary.

CHAPTER FIVE:
SONGS AND STONES

Despite early successes, the timing for the launch of People's Songs could not have been worse.

Recalling the summer of 1946, Seeger said of the organization: "We knew we were being successful when red-baiting articles appeared against us in the leading New York papers. [That] didn't bother us, nor at the time, PAC [the CIO's Political Action Committee]." Early in '46, the organization even managed to pull off a few cooperative ventures with the American Federation of Labor [AFL], this group far more conservative than the CIO. But the brief halcyon days of People's Songs were about to end, and those headlines Seeger thought a sign of the group's "success" were in fact a belle-weather signaling trouble on the horizon. Shortly, as Doris Willens has written, "CIO unions would purge their left wings in a general stampede by organizations to prove their anti-Communism, and People's Songs would become more and more isolated from the labor movement it had hoped to serve."

Within a year of the founding of the organization, the United States Justice Department began formally compiling and publishing a list of groups it considered "un-American," with People's Songs near the top. The CIO passed an anti-Communist resolution in November of '46. Unbeknownst to Seeger and his cohorts, as of March '47 the FBI established regular surveillance of the group who, one internal memo reported "play folksongs ... where the hoity-toity red intellectuals gather."

As Dunaway notes: "In the next two years the Bureau compiled five hundred pages on People's Songs, including stolen and photocopied documents; phone calls recorded without warrants; and infiltration of PSI board meetings." Dunaway concludes with great insight: "The FBI took People's Songs more seriously than the Communist Party did." When People's Artists held its first (and last) national convention in Chicago during October of '47 – a gathering where Seeger was elected Chairman of the Board – a mere 60 people showed up.

*

The organization – mostly in the person of Pete, but often with Paul Robeson on the scene as well – threw itself headlong into the election of 1948, supporting the Progressive Party candidacy of Henry Wallace (FDR's former Vice President and Agriculture Secretary). The candidate denounced the Cold War and was widely criticized as being "Stalin's nominee for President."

In backing Wallace, People's Songs sealed the deal on its divorce from organized labor, since both the AFL and the CIO, after having officially purged Communists from their ranks, refused to back the Progressive Party, instead throwing their support behind the Democrat Truman.

(Some affiliates even went so far as to condemn the Progressive Party as little more than a Communist front.)

It is indeed the case that the Wallace campaign hosted many Communists in significant positions, although the naive Wallace seems to have been oblivious, at least for awhile. As the playwright Lillian Hellman [a friend of both Seeger and Wallace] would recall, a month or so before the election Wallace "asked me if it was true [what the media was saying] that many of the people, the important people, in the Progressive Party were Communists. It was such a surprising question that I laughed and said it most certainly was true." Among those publicly leveling charges of Communist infiltration were H.L. Mencken and Dorothy Thompson. Concurrent with the presidential campaign, the HUAC publicly investigated and embarrassed the Progressive Party with revelations of Communist participation – facts which quickly sank the already foundering ship.

Jeane J. Kirkpatrick (Reagan foreign policy adviser, chief architect of the anti-Communist foreign policy program known as the "Reagan Doctrine," and Ambassador to the United Nations) would remember attending a Columbia University campaign rally "at which Pete Seeger played the banjo, Norman Mailer introduced the candidate and Henry Wallace strode onto the stage with a forthright appeal to political paranoia. 'Now you will be investigated too,' he shouted to the standing-room-only crowd." The "hoity-toity" intellectual Columbia audience cheered, but out on the hustings the campaign was often met by angry mobs and thrown eggs. Wallace's loss at the polls was not just a loss; it was a humiliation. The candidate garnered only 2.4% of the popular vote, finishing in fourth place behind the militant segregationist Strom Thurmond, who ran on the States' Rights Democratic (aka, *Dixiecrat*) ticket.

The commitment of People's Songs to the Progressive campaign not only destroyed its ties to the union movement, but also effectively bankrupted the organization. By the end of 1948, People's Songs was some $12,000 in debt. Within several months the office was closed and the organization dissolved. Not long after, Pete – disappointed in the party and at the same time beginning to realize the crimes being perpetrated by Stalin upon his own people – opted not to renew his membership in the CPA. ("I should have left much earlier," he said later. "It was stupid of me not to.") That summer, he commenced building his cabin in Beacon.

*

In early September, right-wing mobs (aided by complicit police) attacked cars leaving the site of a Cortlandt, NY benefit concert for the Civil Rights Congress – a concert at which Seeger and Paul Robeson had just performed. The KKK (in fact, KKK members within the local police department) and other right-wing organizations had carefully organized themselves for the occasion. Shouts of "go home kikes" and "get out of here niggers" rang out as baseball-sized rocks were hurled and autos jostled. Police and state troopers did nothing. They just looked on, amused. (Paul Robeson Jr., married to a white woman who had accompanied him to the concert, very nearly got lynched.) Seeger saved several of the stones that landed in his station wagon (barely missing his wife and small children, and shattering a window that rained glass down on his son Danny). Taking them home, he cemented the stones into the new fireplace he was building, so as to never forget what was to become known as the second of the *Peekskill Riots*. (An earlier violent eruption had forced the cancellation of the first attempt to mount the concert on August 27th.)

"The Peekskill Riots demonstrate the politically fraught atmosphere of [the] time and the multivalent role that music played in cultural combat." So writes ethnomusicologist Scott Linford. "To the local police … Robeson's music was a loud symbol of Communism and racial equality, a sonic threat … To the violent protesters, it was an anti-American insult that inspired hatred. To the concert-goers, it was a locus of solidarity worth risking bodily harm to hear and, later, in the embattled cars and buses, a font of collective courage and a defense against flung stones."

All of this occurred against the backdrop of the two highly-publicized Hiss-Chambers trials, the first beginning

May 31st and ending in a hung jury on July 7th, and the second to commence November 17th and run until January 21st 1950, ending with the conviction of Hiss on perjury charges – in effect confirming the former high-ranking diplomat's guilt with regard to espionage conducted on behalf of the Soviet Union over a period of many years as a member of the American Communist underground.

In less than a year, Julius and Ethel Rosenberg would be arrested for their role in conspiring to funnel American atomic secrets to the Soviets. Bombastic rhetoric intoned regularly at HUAC sessions routinely painted all political dissenters, civil rights advocates, and workers for social and economic justice, as well as left-leaning artists, writers and musicians, with one broad brush as aligned with traitorous enemies of the American way. Casting all dissent of any kind as Communist-inspired became *de rigueur* – and often a convenient cover for social positions less attractive and stylish than anti-Communism, these for the most part being anti-Semitism and racism against blacks.

Bombastic rhetoric from key sectors of the American *left* did not help matters much. Paul Robeson, for one, provided gun-powder to the other side when he honestly, vehemently, bravely, unapologetically and quite self-destructively insisted before the HUAC that "In Russia I felt for the first time like a full human being. No color prejudice like in Mississippi, no color prejudice like in Washington. It was the first time I felt like a human being.

Where I did not feel the pressure of color as I feel [it] in this Committee today."

Again and again Robeson made public statements to the effect that Soviet Russia had never enslaved his people, lynched his people, segregated his people. " ... all Africa remembers that it was Litvinov who stood alone beside Haile Selassie in Geneva, when Mussolini's sons flew with the blessings of the Pope to drop bombs on Ethiopian women and children," Robeson told a gathering of the National Council of American-Soviet Friendship. "Africa remembers that it was the Soviet Union which fought the attempts of the Smuts to annex Southwest Africa to the slave reservation of the Union of South Africa. ... The Soviet Union is the friend of the African and the West Indian people."

According to Robeson's most astute biographer, Martin Duberman – as well as his son Paul Jr. and others in a position to speak with authority – Robeson knew full well about Stalin's purges against Jews, intellectuals and others (some of them, such as the Yiddish poet Itzik Feffer, Robeson's own good friends), but refused to publicly acknowledge these crimes for fear that to do so would strengthen the hand of reactionary forces in the United States. Looking back, it might well be argued that to be seen at the time as denying undeniable, well-publicized and documented Stalinist barbarities was itself the surest way of buttressing the right wing's fixation on – and restoring their faith in the existence of – a sinister

American fifth column embracing all aspects of society,
including the arts.

AMERICANS.....
DON'T PATRONIZE REDS !!!!

————•————

YOU CAN DRIVE THE REDS OUT OF TELEVISION, RADIO AND HOLLYWOOD.....

THIS TRACT WILL TELL YOU HOW.

WHY WE MUST DRIVE THEM OUT:

1) The REDS have made our Screen, Radio and TV Moscow's most effective Fifth Column in America . . . 2) The REDS of Hollywood and Broadway have always been the chief financial support of Communist propaganda in America . . . 3) OUR OWN FILMS, made by RED Producers, Directors, Writers and STARS, are being used by Moscow in ASIA, Africa, the Balkans and throughout Europe to create hatred of America . . . 4) RIGHT NOW films are being made to craftily glorify MARXISM, UNESCO and ONE-WORLDISM . . . and via your TV Set they are being piped into your Living Room—and are poisoning the minds of your children under your very eyes ! ! !

So REMEMBER — If you patronize a Film made by RED Producers, Writers, Stars and STUDIOS you are aiding and abetting COMMUNISM . . . every time you permit REDS to come into your Living Room VIA YOUR TV SET you are helping MOSCOW and the INTERNATIONALISTS to destroy America ! ! !

CHAPTER SIX:
AMERICA SINGING

In June of 1950, Alan Lomax found himself named in a small book – *Red Channels* – published by the right wing journal *Counterattack*. The little directory listed 151 musicians, writers, actors, and broadcast journalists supposedly involved in exploiting America's entertainment media to advance red agendas. (*Red Channels* also mentioned actors Edward G. Robinson and Burgess Meredith, writers Lillian Hellman and Dorothy Parker, CBS radio personality John Henry Faulk, conductor and composer Leonard Bernstein, and of course Seeger, along with fellow folksingers Burl Ives and Josh White.) The same month of *Red Currents*, June, the Korean War began.

Three months later, Lomax departed for Europe, where he would spend nine years collecting folk music on the Continent, working from a home base in London. Lomax departed New York by ship on September 24th, one day after the McCarran Act – legislation enabling the Federal government to require the registration of individuals and organizations deemed to be "subversive," and empowering the government to take such actions as denying the right to travel – went into effect. (It was under the McCarran Act that Paul Robeson would lose his passport. Pete's father Charles endured the same indignity, this evidently because of his ancient affiliation with the Composers' Collective along with his insidious connection to his son, who also saw his own passport called back in due course.) Within days of Alan's departure, former Columbia professor Duncan Emrich, who now headed the Library of Congress's Archive of American Folk Song, wrote a memorandum informing the FBI of his concern "at the efforts of Communists and Communist sympathizers to infiltrate and gain control of folksinging."

Ironically, despite the rising tide of witch-hunts, Seeger's career as an entertainer was going better than ever. During late '49 he'd formed a new quartet, *The Weavers* (a name inspired by Gerhart Hauptmann's radical play *Die Weber*, about an 1844 uprising of Silesian weavers). The group – consisting of Pete, Lee Hays, a young People's Songs vet by the name of Fred Hellerman, and the beautifully-voiced Ronnie Gilbert – could not have been more different from the random, chaotic Almanac Singers.

Their sound – though true to folk roots – was tight, well-rehearsed, sophisticated *and commercial*. A very high level of musicianship prevailed. They became known for their carefully-crafted harmonies and for Pete's and Fred's gently interwoven instrumental duets on banjo and guitar: the most precise melodic craftsmanship. The Weavers brought fresh life to ancient ballads, and introduced new material as well, with politics barely present, if at all.

(When Seeger suggested including "If I Had a Hammer" in the set list, the other three Weavers vetoed the idea.) They even looked the part. Gone were the bluejeans and workshirts of the Almanacs. The men dressed in matching jackets. Ronnie wore evening dresses.

Opening at Max Gordon's popular Village Vanguard nightclub Christmas week 1949, the Weavers were to remain in residence for a full six months. After Alan Lomax brought Carl Sandburg to hear them play, the old poet made a statement much quoted in the press: "When I hear America singing, the Weavers are there. [They are] out of the grass roots of America. I salute them." Reviews in *Variety* and elsewhere praised their smooth, ingratiating performances, including Lee Hays's witty chatter and storytelling in between numbers. They quickly became *au courant* – the act to catch, the toast of the cocktail crowd, the darlings of the smart set.

A recording contract with Decca promptly followed, with famed orchestra leader Gordon Jenkins producing the group. Their first single – a beautiful reworking of the Israeli soldiers' tune "Tzena, Tzena" – charted immediately upon its appearance in June, with the "B" side of "Goodnight Irene" (written by Lee's and Pete's old friend, the great black folksinger and twelve-string guitarist Leadbelly) proving just as popular. Tours took them to Ciro's in Hollywood, Houston's Shamrock House, and casinos in Reno and Las Vegas – places where the abstinent Puritan Seeger felt quite out of his element.

(During the Shamrock House engagement, he spent his daylight hours collecting folksongs at a nearby Texas prison.)

In New York, along with the Village Vanguard, they also played at Max Gordon's Blue Angel and other posh venues, being paid sometimes as much as $4000 per week. Milton Berle featured them on his television show. At a casino in Vegas they double-billed with The Three Stooges, and at Baltimore's Hippodrome with Yvonne De Carlo. In Detroit, after much debate, they performed at a nightclub that refused to serve blacks. And they continued to turn out hit records, including such subversive ditties as "On Top of Old Smokey," "Kisses Sweater Than Wine," and Woody Guthrie's "So Long, It's Been Good to Know Yuh." (In this, their heyday, the Weavers sold more than 4 million records worldwide.)

Friends on the left criticized the Weavers for bowing to commercialism and sacrificing their topical material. Punning on the name *Weavers* and the term *fellow travelers*, some lefties called them the *Unravellers*. In the newly launched *Sing Out!* Magazine – which Hays and Seeger had quietly helped finance – editor and party-loyalist Irwin Silber denounced the quartet for "white-washing" Leadbelly's music (even though royalties from the hit recording of "Goodnight Irene" had rescued Leadbelly's widow Martha from abject poverty and a job as a laundress).

To many it seemed the Weavers had "sold out." They were pawns of the capitalists, traitors willing to prostitute their music and make it into a tool to soothe and entertain rather than incite. They were not unlike scabs. They were well-dressed minstrels singing to the court, entertaining lords, ladies and their sycophants while beyond the castle walls surfs toiled and suffered.

Nevertheless, Pete Kameron, the young assistant to their newly acquired manager Harold Leventhal, insisted they continue to stay away from things political, not only in their repertoire but in their private lives. No more picket lines. No more benefits for defense funds. Once their fame was solidified they'd be able to do whatever they wanted, however Kameron and Leventhal did not want them to unwittingly cut their careers off in the bud. They urged the Weavers – particularly the increasingly restive Seeger – to look at the big picture: the long-term good.

Despite the compromises and supposed abandonment of principle that so troubled Silber and others, the Weavers – with their rapidly rising fame – became a juicy target for red-baiters. At first the issue was more of a nuisance than anything else – just loose, imprecise rumors easily batted away by Lee with a few wry comments made entertainingly to querying reporters. In September of 1950 – during the same week Lomax departed for Europe – a generally complimentary *Time* Magazine profile of the group casually noted that several of the singers had previously been affiliated with the "red-tinged" and now defunct People's Songs, but no-one seemed to take much notice.

Only later on, during the spring and summer of 1951, did things begin to get ugly. Van Camp's Pork and Beans quietly withdrew an offer to sponsor a Weavers-hosted weekly network television program, and a booked appearance on Dave Garroway's morning television show mysteriously became unbooked, with no reason given. In September, a performance at the Ohio State Fair was abruptly canceled just hours before the scheduled show, after Governor Frank Lausche received information directly from J. Edgar Hoover concerning the Weavers, their known political affiliations in the past, and their suspected political affiliations in the present.

One week later, an expose in the *New York-World Telegram* quoted from the same supposedly confidential FBI reports. *Variety* and *Downbeat* took notice. Remarkably, it was even the case that the Congressional Internal Security Subcommittee took up the question of whether or not the Weavers had ever acted in violation of Title 18 of the U.S. Code, sections 2383: inciting and/or advocating rebellion, insurrection, or seditious conspiracy. (No action was brought, but the resultant publicity proved to be action enough.)

During the first week of February 1952, 26-year-old Harvey Matusow – an ex-Communist who had once worked in the offices of People's Songs – testified before the HUAC that three of the Weavers (Pete, Fred and

Ronnie) were active members of the CPA, and that Lee had once been. At about the same time, Matusow became an editor at *Counterattack*. (Three years later, in his book *False Witness*, Matusow admitted to having been a paid informant who, at the behest of Roy Cohn, lied to incriminate numerous musicians, artists and writers. As a result of these admissions, Matusow wound up spending almost three years in a Federal prison on the charge of perjury.)

On the very day of Matusow's testimony, the manager of the Yankee Inn outside of Akron, where the Weavers were in the midst of a several-day engagement, canceled their contract effective immediately. Although the group continued to tour on and off through most of '52 and early '53, their venues became less and less desirable, their salaries took a nosedive, and Decca declined to renew their contract. As of spring '53 the Weavers took themselves off the road for a "sabbatical." June saw the execution of Julius and Ethel Rosenberg.

CHAPTER SEVEN:
A LIGHT BURNING LOW

Ironically, Seeger found the initial net result of the
blacklist to be quite liberating – politically, artistically,
personally and spiritually. No longer bound within the
straightjacket of "success," he was free to perform
whenever he wanted, for whomever he wanted, wherever
he wanted, without fear of commercial reprisal. That ax
had already fallen.

He had never been comfortable with the compromises
– both musically and politically – involved with being a
top-40 performer. He'd tolerated the waltz-like orchestral
backing Gordon Jenkins had arranged for the Weavers
recording of "Goodnight Irene." He'd allowed Pete
Kameron to talk him out of performing at left-wing events
(although he, as well as the other Weavers, still managed
to slip in a few, surreptitiously sneaking more under the
radar of their own management than under the radar of
the FBI). He'd put up with the smoke-filled casinos – their
liquor and gaming. He'd sublimated what he considered
the better angels of his nature to the cause of fame and
achieving a celebrity which he'd hoped would empower
him to be of more use to the causes he held dear – only to
find himself enjoined from participation in those causes
lest his celebrity be ripped away from him. Spiritually he'd

felt empty. For the moment, he was at least in part pleased to be done with "success" as traditionally defined.

Although this is hard for most people to understand, great financial reward had never been and would never be a goal for either Toshi or Pete Seeger. The idea of wealth quite literally meant nothing to them so long as there was a roof over their heads and their children were fed. Through the 1960s, 1970s and thereafter, as money rolled in from such Seeger-penned hits as "Where Have All the Flowers Gone?" (the Kingston Trio as well as Marlene Dietrich), "Turn! Turn! Turn!" (the Byrds) and "If I Had a Hammer" (Peter, Paul and Mary), as concert fees escalated and a lucrative Columbia recording contract began delivering significant returns, the Seegers would continue to live in their humble, hand-hewn home on the mountainside, Pete would continue to chop wood for their heat, and cars and trucks would continue to be driven into the ground before being replaced.

Numerous concerts were benefits. Seeger routinely sang for free at political rallies and protests, traveling to them at his own expense. And as their income rose, generous contributions – most of them anonymous – flowed into organizations the Seegers thought important. Thus Toshi and Pete shunned the embarrassment of riches in exchange for what William James once called "the extravagance of human tenderness." (Seeger often quoted Christ's words that it was easier for a camel to pass through the eye of a needle than for a rich man to enter the

Kingdom of Heaven.) "Prestige is much overrated," he would write in *Seventeen* Magazine, contributing his thoughts to a monthly column wherein well known personages gave advice to young people. "The celebrity business is for the birds. Respectability is nice, but consider: whom do you most want to respect you? Money is like air or water. You need a certain amount to live. Beyond that, who wants to be a dog in the manger?" He also warned against the tyranny of possessions. Gather too many and "they possess you." As Don McLean once noted, Pete "tried to stay hungry even when he didn't have to. I've often wondered why anyone would do that. But I can see why, from his perspective, it's very important."

Toshi and Pete Seeger quite literally lived for the higher good, to which they devoted their lives. James alluded to these types of selfless individuals in *The Varieties of Religious Experience.* "Like the single drops which sparkle in the sun as they are flung far ahead of the advancing edge of a wave-crest or of a flood, they show the way and are forerunners. The world [has not yet caught up with their sensibilities], so they often seem in the midst of the world's affairs to be preposterous. Yet they are the impregnators of the world, vivifiers and animators of potentialities of goodness which, but for them, would lie forever dormant. It is not possible to be quite as mean as we naturally are, when they have passed before us. One fire kindles another; and without that over-trust in human worth which they show, the rest of us would lie in spiritual stagnancy."

One thinks of the Catholic anarchist Dorothy Day and her Catholic Worker Movement, Jane Addams of Hull House, abolitionist William Lloyd Garrison in his impoverished loft getting out countless (generally ignored) editions of *The Liberator,* and many others whose candles, through the centuries, have burned low in the windows of the human firmament, casting little lights which, despite their smallness, have been visible from afar. Those who, like me, have known the Seegers through the decades will understand that I do not over-state or romanticize when I speak of them in this context. A priest's or rabbi's devotion to God, this was the level of their devotion to social, economic and eventually environmental justice. This is the truth – no matter how saccharine the description might seem.

In his later years, Seeger would argue against the "great man" theory of history, and big movements in general, instead insisting upon the importance of a multitude of small acts. Small was beautiful. Big was not. One's own individual principle, if followed truly and adhered to unwaveringly, could stand not only as a guidepost and example for others, but also as a demarcation line in the course of history. Rosa Parks's single solitary personal act of civil disobedience in 1955 – when she refused to give up her seat to a white customer on a segregated Montgomery, Alabama bus – resounded around the world, thus reviving a fire of discontent that had been left too long to smolder. Seeger told a friend, quoting one of his favorite spirituals, that he hoped his own "little light" shined at least a bit, leading others who wished to see down a road that was worth traveling.

Throughout most of his career, Seeger frequently likened his work to that of one of his heroes, Johnny Appleseed (John Chapman, 1774-1845), the itinerant Swedenborgian preacher, wanderer and abolitionist who voluntarily spent most of his life homeless, on the road, planting orchards across the countryside. Seeger viewed his songs as seeds which he sowed wherever and whenever he could. Chapman lived the truth of his Swedenborgian faith which said all who did good would be accepted by the Lord into Heaven, as God was goodness itself, and that doing good conjoined one with God.

In matters of faith, Seeger himself seems to have been rather ecumenical. While singing at a gathering of the Long Island West District of the United Methodist Church in the mid 1970s, Seeger told attendees he supposed he could best define his religious philosophy as Swedenborgian. Much later, in 1992, he joined the Community Church of New York, a Unitarian Universalist congregation. Onetime Beacon neighbor Elizabeth West remembers the Seegers regularly attending Quaker Friends' meetings in the late fifties and early sixties. "Pete's daughter, who was about my age, used to arrive in a

simple shift and without shoes! She came to church
barefoot. ... I understood that there was an integrity and
depth of commitment inherent in this little freedom his
daughter enjoyed that has inspired me all my life." (Had
the Seegers lived in Westminster, Maryland instead of
Beacon, NY, they would have been attending the same
Quaker meetings as did Whittaker Chambers.)

During the early fifties, in the wake of the Weavers,
Seeger benefited from the fact that the purveyors of the
blacklist, in their quest for big fish and big headlines,
continued to train their guns on venues and institutions he
was quite happy to eschew. He did not truly *want* the type
of work being denied him: the ritzy clubs, the top-40
charts, the network television programs. In this period,
though financially strapped, Seeger found his artistic
balance in performing for grade schools and at summer
camps for an honorarium of $25 or sometimes even less.
He reveled in teaching kids "This Land is Your Land" and
"Kumbaya" – thus, unwittingly, breaking ground for what
would become the folk boom of the sixties. (The ten year
old of 1953 would be the twenty year old of 1963.)

He also toured small colleges in the hinterlands,
where progressive faculty knew his story and cleared his
way (thus pioneering what would become the college
concert circuit). And he cut disk after disk for Folkways
Records (a highly respected yet hole-in-the-wall label
owned and managed by his friend Moe Asch, for whom
Leadbelly and Guthrie had also recorded). These records

were the antithesis of commercial: *American Industrial Ballads, Champlain Valley Songs* and so forth.

Asch was also not at all averse to topical material, giving Seeger free rein to record whatever songs he saw fit. On *Love Songs for Friends and Foes* he included "If I Had a Hammer" and Ed McCurdy's pacifist anthem "Strangest Dream," along with the spirituals "Down by the Riverside" and "I'm Gonna Walk and Talk with Jesus." They were, to him, all of the same fabric. Moe's records were sold to school libraries and through a very loosely-knit network of specialty record shops at home and abroad. Instead of millions, each title sold in the hundreds. A significant chunk of the business was via mail-order to folk aficionados in the States, Canada and Europe.

Seeger's light continued to burn low.

CHAPTER EIGHT:
THE LAST FREE PLACE IN
AMERICA

One very important thing to note about the HUAC hearings of the 1950s was their backward looking, historical focus. In the standard question asked by the HUAC and by Joseph McCarthy on the Senate side: "Are you now or have you ever been a member of the Communist Party?" the key phrase was the latter half: *have you ever been.*

The enfeebled "open" CPA, after having been abandoned by the unions in the late 1940s, was on life-support well before the inquisitors of the 1950s ever really got around to the brunt of their work. By the time they did, as Norman Mailer put it, "American Communists [were] as dangerous to the security of the United States as the last American buffalo." They were also greatly diminished in numbers, with many members of the open party – Seeger among them – having left the ranks quite a while before receiving subpoenas (in Seeger's case, six years).

As for the underground Communist network, it had been largely decimated by the revelations of former operative Whitaker Chambers in 1948, the two Hiss trials, and the prosecution of the Rosenbergs. (Joe McCarthy himself was, by the start of 1955, "old news," having been censured by the Senate in the wake of the Army McCarthy Hearings. In retrospect, the disgraced senator's quest to unearth Communist infiltration of the Federal government appeared to most as little more than an extended exercise in vile self-promotion.)

In fact, to a great extent, the espionage underground had been at least hobbled since *well before* 1948. Sam Tanenhaus has discussed what he calls Chambers's "outdated" testimony: "He described his purpose as 'eradicating Communism in the United States', as though this were 1938, not 1948. ... Chambers implied Hiss still posed a danger to national security when the man had been out of government since 1947. Like so many ex-Communists, Chambers was cocooned in a bygone period, that of his own underground exploits, the vanished era of 1936 – of Spain, the show trials, the Popular Front ... ." By the time Seeger was called to testify, Stalin had been dead two years.

Those appearing before the HUAC had three options. The first was to be a "cooperating" or "friendly" witness. This involved admitting past wrongful associations, naming names of those with whom one had been associated, and thus – usually – gaining favor and getting one's name off the blacklist. Cooperating witnesses could be "born again," as it were. The second path was to remain silent by invoking one's right (via the Fifth Amendment) not to bear witness against oneself. In this way one could be unfriendly and uncooperative without risking a citation for contempt of Congress. (Those who chose this approach were popularly labeled "Fifth Amendment Communists." They remained blacklisted, unemployable, and generally without sympathy – but they were immune to prosecution. In short, those who took the Fifth did not take it lightly, and were being quite brave.) The third and most treacherous option was to refuse to answer questions while at the same time refusing to take the Fifth – in effect, to question the very legitimacy of the Committee and invite prosecution for contempt.

The entire tableau of an HUAC hearing resembled and had the same tone as a show trial under Stalin: both were one-sided theatrical events contrived to humiliate, violate, embarrass and condemn those suspected of political thoughts and actions of which the state disapproved. All were guilty before they walked in the door – the only thing that mattered was how they conducted themselves (whether or not they genuflected) before the Committee. To the most acute observers, it seemed political dissent was dealt with in essentially the same way on both sides of the Iron Curtain, with contrarians denied rights, ostracized, forbidden to travel and at times threatened with even graver consequences.

Former friends of Hays and Seeger – among them the singer/actor Burl Ives and the singer Josh White, both one-time Almanac associates – chose to surrender and genuflect, cooperating and naming names of those whom they knew *or even suspected* of having Communist affiliations in the present or the past. Thus they restored their careers at the expense of onetime colleagues. (Ives, in particular, named Seeger, who subsequently wrote in *Sing Out!* that Ives had done this purely "because he felt it was the only way to preserve his lucrative contracts; and that makes his action all the more despicable." Seeger went on to compare Ives to Falstaff, the Shakespearean character who was "gross, gargantuan, talented and clever; he was also not quite intelligent enough to be honorable." After White testified, Seeger drew a picture of a guitar broken in two with the intention of mailing it to White. Then he thought twice. Years later he still had the drawing in his desk drawer.)

Lillian Hellman – whose long-time companion, the mystery writer Dashiell Hammett (of Sam Spade fame) had gone to jail in 1951 rather than reveal the names of contributors to the Civil Rights Conference – took the Fifth before the Committee, saying "I cannot and will not cut my conscience to fit this year's fashions … ." Hellman had been willing to testify freely about her own past, but was advised that if she did not take the Fifth regarding herself she would then be forced to testify about others or else risk a citation for contempt. Hellman said she had no intention of bringing "bad trouble to people who, in my past association with them, were completely innocent of any talk or any action that was disloyal or subversive." Paul Robeson likewise took the Fifth, as did many others. Comedic actor Zero Mostel invoked the amendment by holding up five fingers and wiggling them at Committee members. Seeger's friend, actor Howard DaSilva (named in previous testimony by actor Robert Taylor) took the Fifth as well, as did another Seeger friend, *Wizard of Oz* lyricist E.Y. (Yip) Harburg.

The third and most treacherous path for a witness was, as previously mentioned, to forego the Fifth Amendment and remain silent on the "strength" of the First Amendment, which guarantees the rights of free speech and association. This had been the stance of the Hollywood Ten. In 1949, after the Supreme Court refused to entertain appeals of their convictions for contempt of Congress based on their assertion of the First Amendment, all ten went to prison. (Screenwriter Ring Lardner Jr. bumped into his former HUAC interrogator, one-time Committee chair J. Parnell Thomas, as a fellow inmate at Danbury Federal Prison, Thomas having been convicted in a kickback bribery scheme unrelated to his work with the HUAC.) The down-shot of these and similar court cases was that anyone refusing to speak solely on the basis of the First Amendment could confidently expect indictment, conviction and jail-time.

*

Lee Hays received his subpoena just a few days before Pete. Hays was to appear at the U.S. District Courthouse, Foley Square, on August 16th, 1955, and Seeger two days later. Hays took the Fifth Amendment, resigning himself to continued blacklisting and demonization.

The bulk of the Committee's questions focused on one particular song – "Wasn't That a Time!" – written by Hays and Walter Lowenfels in 1948 as a direct protest against what the authors considered to be the un-American activities of the un-American activities inquisitors. The song compared those who refused to cooperate to the patriotic heroes of Valley Forge and Gettysburg, and criticized contemporary "informers" who worked for "Judas pay" helping "gangs in Congress [have] their way." The chorus declared with regard to Valley Forge and Gettysburg: "Wasn't that a time to try the soul of man; Wasn't that a terrible time!" With regard to the contemporary dilemma, it declared "Isn't this a time to *free* the soul of man; Isn't this a *wonderful* time!"

In this way Hays and Lowenfels harkened back to Thomas Paine's first essay in his revolutionary manifesto *The American Crisis*, with its eloquent and profound observation that "These are the times that try men's souls. The summer soldier and the sunshine patriot will, in this crisis, shrink from the service of their country; but he that stands by it now, deserves the love and thanks of man and woman. Tyranny, like hell, is not easily conquered; yet we have this consolation with us, that the harder the conflict, the more glorious the triumph. What we obtain too cheap, we esteem too lightly: it is dearness only that gives every thing its value. Heaven knows how to put a proper price upon its goods; and it would be strange indeed if so celestial an article as FREEDOM should not be highly rated."

Two days after Hays, it was Seeger's turn to confront the HUAC. Seeger's chief questioners were Gordon H. Scherer (R-Ohio) and Frank S. Tavenner Jr., chief counsel for the Committee. (An important note here: Gore Vidal and others have written that Scherer was at the time a supporter of the John Birch Society. This would have been a neat trick, since the Society was not founded until December 1958. That being said, it is worthwhile to always remember that history, like life, is a complicated thing. When the time came, Scherer was in fact – along with William F. Buckley Jr. and other prominent conservatives – an outspoken critic of the Society. Still, he pursued Seeger and other unfriendly HUAC witnesses with tenacious and vitriolic vigor.)

Seeger's attorney, Paul L. Ross (the same attorney who represented Hays), accompanied him and advised him to take the Fifth, as had Harold Leventhal. Knowing full well what he was doing and asking for, Pete refused. Instead he simply told the Committee: "I am not going to answer any questions as to my associations, my philosophical or religious beliefs, or how I voted in any election or any of these private affairs. I think these are very improper questions for any American to be asked, especially under such compulsion as this. ... I love my country very dearly, and I greatly resent this implication that some of the places that I have sung and some of the people that I have known, and some of my opinions, whether they are religious or philosophical, or I might be a vegetarian, make me any less of an American."

On this basis Seeger repeatedly refused to answer questions about where and for whom he had sung, what he had sung, benefits and organizations he'd been involved with, people he'd worked with, and publications for which he'd written. Repeatedly he responded: "I have given you my answer." A brief quotation from the transcript gives a good idea of the overall tone of the proceedings.

> MR. TAVENNER: ... My purpose in asking you these questions, Mr. Seeger, is to determine whether or not, in accordance with the plan of the Communist Party as outlined by Mr. [Elia] Kazan and Mr. George Hall, you were performing a valuable service to the Communist Party, and if that was the way they attempted to use you.
>
> MR. SEEGER: Is that a question, sir?
>
> MR. TAVENNER: That is my explanation to you, with the hope that you will give the Committee some light on that subject.
>
> MR. SEEGER: No, my answer is the same as before.

MR. TAVENNER: Did you also perform and entertain at various functions held by front organizations, such as the American Youth for Democracy? I have here photostatic copies of the *Daily Worker* indicating such programs were conducted in Detroit in 1952, at Greenwich Village on May 10, 1947, and again at another place in March of 1948. Did you entertain at functions under the auspices of the American Youth for Democracy?

(Witness consulted with counsel.)

MR. SEEGER: The answer is the same, and I take it that you are not interested in all of the different places that I have sung. Why don't you ask me about the churches and schools and other places?

MR. TAVENNER: That is very laudable, indeed, and I wish only that your activities had been confined to those areas. If you were acting for the Communist Party at these functions, we want to know it. We want to determine just what the Communist Party plan was.

MR. SCHERER: Witness, you have indicated that you are perfectly willing to tell us about all of these innumerable functions at which you entertained, but why do you refuse to tell us about the functions that Mr. Tavenner inquires about?

MR. SEEGER: No, sir, I said that I should be glad to tell you about all of the songs that I have sung, because I feel that the songs are the clearest explanation of what I do believe in, as a musician, and as an American.

MR. SCHERER: Didn't you just say that you sang before various religious groups, school groups?

MR. SEEGER: I have said it and I will say it again, and I have sung for perhaps-

(Witness consulted with counsel.)

MR. SCHERER: You are willing to tell us about those groups?

MR. SEEGER: I am saying voluntarily that I have sung for almost every religious group in the country, from Jewish and Catholic, and Presbyterian and Holy Rollers and Revival Churches, and I do this voluntarily. I have sung for many, many different groups-and it is hard for perhaps one person to believe, I was looking back over the twenty years or so that I have sung around these forty-eight states, that I have sung in so many different places.

MR. SCHERER: Did you sing before the groups that Mr. Tavenner asked you about?

MR. SEEGER: I am saying that my answer is the same as before. I have told you that I sang for everybody.

When grilled on the song "Wasn't That a Time!," Seeger refused to answer questions but offered to perform the song for the Committee – an offer that was abruptly and gruffly rebuffed. Later on, after being excused from the witness chair, Seeger broke out his banjo and sang the song in the hallway outside the hearing room for reporters and television cameras. As Doris Willens reports: "Harold Leventhal told Pete and Lee it was a hell of a way to get a song on the air." Earl Robinson – composer of "I Dreamed I Saw Joe Hill Last Night," "The House I Live In," and many other songs – caught the television coverage and wrote Seeger: "I had many twinges of conscience at being on vacation and enjoying myself out in God's country while you guys were going through the ordeal. But no doubt my time will come. The old subpoenas-envy again."

In the HUAC's medieval theater of ritual humiliation, contrition and absolution, it did not matter that the facts Seeger and others were asked to either confirm or deny were already to a large degree matters of public record. Consider: It is the rare political rally, musical concert or fundraiser that is not widely publicized in the hope that someone might actually attend. There is nary a protest march one might perform before, or petition one might sign, in the process of which one might also remain anonymous. There isn't a song that can be sung in public without someone hearing it.

In a sense, the Committee *relied* on unfriendly witnesses taking the Fifth (or standing on the First) Amendment to refrain from answering, in order to cast an otherwise unobtainable sinister shadow over relatively innocent things. But such recalcitrance – especially principled stands based on the First Amendment, which in essence questioned the very legitimacy of the inquisition – nevertheless demanded punishment in the absence of contrition. This was the vital denouement with which the theatrical needed to close in order to be a success. Such was the balance of the ceremonial dance being enacted. For Fifth Amendment Communists, the denouement was continued blacklisting. For others like Seeger, it meant something more – the difference between purgation by the whip and purgation by fire.

A few months after Seeger's testimony, Fred Hellerman and Harold Leventhal paid a visit to Woody Guthrie (suffering from the early stages of Huntington's Disease, which triggered occasional psychotic episodes) at the New Jersey State Psychiatric Hospital, Greystone Park. When they inquired of Woody how he was doing, he replied: "You don't have to worry about me. I'm worried about how *you* boys are doing. Out there, if you guys say you are Communists, they'll put you in jail. But in here, I can get up there and say 'I'm a Communist' and all they say is 'Ah, he's crazy.' You know, this is the last free place in America."

Shortly, after being informed by Guthrie's doctors that Guthrie suffered from "Huntington's Chorea, a chronic neurological condition ... a deteriorating disease with no known cure," the special agent in charge of the FBI's New York Office recommended to J. Edgar Hoover that the folksinger be removed from the bureau's watch-list.

CHAPTER NINE:
PURGATORY

Increasingly frustrated (and downright annoyed) by the blacklist, the cigar-chomping and short-fused Harold Leventhal decided – in the wake of Hays's and Seeger's interrogations – that it was time for positive offensive action against the blacklisters. After conferring with his clients, Leventhal took the significant financial risk of renting Carnegie Hall for what was billed as a triumphant Weavers reunion concert: a "Holiday Concert" to be held Christmas Eve, 1955. If no-one would hire the Weavers, they would hire themselves. It was the hope (and, indeed, the expectation) that they could count on the support of their core politically-sympathetic fans in what was, after all, their "home city."

Harold's hunch proved correct. Tickets sold out within hours of being put on sale. Performance-wise, the Weavers had never been better. The concert proved both an artistic and commercial success. Shortly after, Harold booked Carnegie for a Spring return appearance while also fielding phone calls from venues and producers across the country who were interested enough – and brave enough – to want to mount Weavers performances in their cities. Harold recorded the Christmas concert off Carnegie Hall's house sound-system, and eventually (after about a year and a half of attempts) found a small but respected label –

Vanguard – willing to release the disk, the first of several the Weavers would record for the firm.

The Vanguard Recording Society, founded in 1950 by brothers Maynard and Seymour Solomon, had started off with classical recordings before branching out into jazz and eventually folk. With practically no commercial radio play, the firm had little to lose in challenging the blacklist. The Solomon brothers also signed Paul Robeson. The tiny label found itself learning through experience with a crash-course in mass marketing when, quite unexpectedly, the Christmas concert turned into a commercial hit. September of 1957 saw the record at #3 in *Variety's* list of bestsellers, with the latest Sinatra record at #1 and the soundtrack for the film *Around the World in Eighty Days* at #2.

For a period of several years after Christmas '55, the Weavers played a succession of dates across the country – wherever Harold could find a profitable crack in the wall of red-baiting. Most of these were venues the Weavers (especially Pete) liked enormously. No more noisy casinos, where they were still quite happily not welcome. No more boozy nightclubs, where they were still quite happily not welcome. Just concert halls in urban areas and the occasional college show. Not only were audiences attentive and appreciative, but the group no longer felt inhibited with regard to their set-lists. Along with their standard tight arrangements of traditional folk tunes, they also performed political material. (Their 1958 Vanguard album *The Weavers on Tour* included "Wasn't That a Time!") Newspaper reviewers fawned. But all was not calm.

A stink-bomb set off by right-wingers delayed a May 1956 concert at Chicago's Orchestra Hall, with 5000 people in attendance. Two months later, on July 26th, Seeger and seven others (among them playwright Arthur Miller, who had not only taken a First Amendment stand but as well criticized the HUAC with his 1953 play *The Crucible*, ostensibly about the Salem witch hunts) found themselves cited by the House of Representatives for contempt, in a vote of 373 to 9. Exactly eight months after the House vote, on March 26th 1957, a federal grand jury indicted Seeger on ten counts of contempt. Traveling to Foley Square once more, and pleading not-guilty, he was released on $1000 bail with the understanding (negotiated by Paul Ross) that he would notify the federal district attorney whenever traveling out of New York's Southern District, which was almost always.

Around this time, on a flight to a performance, Pete penned a song he did not at first think very much of:

"Where Have All the Flowers Gone?" He recorded the piece in 1958 for eventual release on what became the 1960 Folkways album *The Rainbow Quest*, but did not regularly perform the number. It was also in this period, the late 1950s, that he wrote his other best known song, "Turn! Turn! Turn!" with its lyrics adapted from *Ecclesiastes*: "To everything there is a season, and a time for every purpose under Heaven." Once again not particularly impressed, he did not bother to record this until the Columbia album *The Bitter and the Sweet*, released January 1963.

*

Although there had been genuinely lean times for two or so years in the early fifties (particularly '54 and '55), the fact is Seeger's lack of work during the mid-to-late fifties has been mythologized to the point of inaccuracy. Despite the blacklist, which kept him off television and off a major label, he still kept quite busy between his solo commitments and his Weavers commitments. In addition to recording with the Weavers, he continued to record as a solo artist for little Folkways, with several of his records – especially three children's albums of the period, plus *American Favorite Ballads* (1957) – proving extraordinarily popular. And he had steady solo work on the college circuit. Between preparing for his upcoming court case and balancing family with career, Seeger burned the proverbial

candle at both ends. He felt quite stretched. Something had
to give.

By the spring of 1958, feeling confident about his solo
prospects, he'd decided to quit the Weavers. Although
long contemplated by Seeger, the break finally came over
participation of the group in a TV commercial for L&M
Cigarettes. Pete, who frowned on smoking and whose
mother-in-law was at the time dying from lung cancer, did
not want to take the job. The other Weavers – all of them
smokers, as was Toshi for that matter – insisted they
needed the rare television exposure, and the pay.
Outvoted, Pete bowed to the majority and filmed the spot.
Then, seizing the excuse, he resigned, recommending the
Weavers replace him with ace banjo and guitar picker Erik
Darling, formerly of the hit group the Tarriers. (The taking
on of Darling introduced a more than interesting political
curve. As Pete well knew, Darling was a staunch
libertarian conservative and admirer of Ayn Rand.)

Seeger's solo concerts were frequently picketed, but
rarely stopped. Publicity generated when right-wing
groups protested an upcoming appearance served as free
advertising and helped generate, rather than depress,
ticket sales. Attempts to silence Seeger maximized already-
existing support among progressives. In this atmosphere,
every concert became more than a mere performance: each
became a symbolic victory, another battle won in an
ongoing struggle for free speech. Pete always made it a
point to sing "Wasn't That a Time!" He also took an old

German protest song – "Die Gedanken Sind Frei"
("Thoughts are Free") – and made it a regular part of his
program. "My thoughts will not cater, to duke or dictator
… " said the lyric. Then came the key verse, loaded with
meaning with regard to Seeger's much-publicized
situation:

> *And should tyrants take me and throw me in prison,*
> *My thoughts will burst free like flowers in season,*
> *Foundations will crumble, and structures will tumble,*
> *And free men will cry: Die Gedanken Sind Frei!*

"The first time I ever got involved in anything that
could be called controversial," Arlo Guthrie remembers,
"was when my class in the fifth or sixth grade took a trip
to hear a Pete Seeger concert. I was going to school in
Brooklyn, and the class went to the venue in a little school
bus, and outside the concert, the John Birch Society was
picketing. They had all these pamphlets and they were
yelling, 'Pete is a Commie,' and calling him all kinds of
names. I walked up to one of the John Birch Society
members and asked, 'Is this really true?' He said, 'Oh, yes,'
and I said, 'Give me those pamphlets. I'm going to help
you out.' They gave me and my classmates all of the
pamphlets and we just put them in our pockets and
walked into the venue, so there were no more pamphlets
for them to give out." Local cells of the Birch Society could
buy standard issue Pete Seeger pamphlets – headlined

Identified Communist Seeger Sings and emblazoned with a hammer and sickle – by the gross from the national office. Fans routinely took the proffered publication and then continued on into the concert, unfazed. After the performance, a smiling Seeger would autograph them.

In July of '58, the Detroit Arts Commission sought to ban a scheduled October Seeger concert sponsored by the Detroit Labor Forum at the Detroit Institute of Arts auditorium. The grounds the Commission cited were that a typical Seeger performance was not in fact a musical concert but rather a political rally, and as such not allowed under the rules of use for the auditorium. Had this decision been allowed to stand, it would have set a very dangerous precedent, laying the philosophical and legal groundwork for all political music to be banned from a number of the most important concert stages across the country. The Detroit Labor forum took the case to court, and for once a federal authority – in the form of a circuit court judge – sided with Seeger, ruling that singers were singers, and politicians politicians. Seeger qualified as the former, and would be allowed to proceed.

In San Diego, the Board of Education insisted Seeger sign a loyalty oath before being allowed to sing in a high school auditorium that had been rented by a liberal organization for the occasion. After much debate, and much protest, the Board overturned this decision and the concert was allowed to proceed (before a packed house). A brief 1959 tour of England – for which he had to obtain a

special limited passport since his own standard-issue
passport had been revoked – provided a welcome respite
from such fights.

*

No matter what went on outside concert halls, it was
during this period that Seeger came into his own as a
uniquely stylized solo concert performer. The message of a
Pete Seeger concert wasn't just political, it was also cultural
– and articulated most often through action rather than
rhetoric. Seeger saw each of his concerts as a blow against
pre-packaged, homogenized mass entertainment. In this
respect, Seeger concerts became grand exercises in
participatory art. Although he interspersed ballads and
instrumentals which leveraged his exceptional skill as a
virtuoso banjo picker and twelve-string guitar stylist, he
saw his main business as joining with his audience in song
as choir-director, teacher and missionary.

The ritual of the typical Pete Seeger performance
involved community-building. Strangers in adjacent
auditorium seats became a united force, in communion
rendering "Jacob's Ladder," "Amazing Grace," and other
timeless masterpieces whittled not by Tin Pan Alley, but
by a succession of anonymous amateurs over the course of
centuries – the so-called "folk process." An air of
enthusiasm and warmth – an almost mystical elevation –
dominated, as it might at a revival meeting.

This to Seeger represented the highest of art – art riddled with meanings and messages writ both large and small: the beauty and meaning and message of many voices together singing; the beauty and meaning and message of songs and anthems carved over time by many hands, evolving and traveling on like a mighty river; the dignity, grace, strength and creativity of common people standing revealed both in composition and performance, and in a manner that created not dissonance but harmony.

Writing in *Time*, Richard Corliss commented on Seeger's astonishing ability to turn a concert audience into a "Mormon Tabernacle Campfire." As Bod Dylan recalls, "Seeger had this amazing ability to look at a group of people and make them all sing a part [soprano, alto, tenor, bass] of a song and he would make an orchestration out of a simple little song with everybody singing. Whether you wanted to or not, you found yourself singing a part and it would be beautiful." In such surroundings, Seeger was both maestro and minister – and completely in his element.

Every once in a while, even the dark wall of the television blacklist gave way. In February of 1960, Seeger performed several songs on Hugh Hefner's "Playboy After Dark." This was one of the country's first nationally syndicated television programs. As the sole syndicator, Hefner had final say on all talent. Not being a fan of the red-baiters, and with no corporate heads to answer to, "Hef" was happy to invite Seeger on. The venue was not exactly Pete's kind of thing, but Harold urged him to do it, if only just to make the point that he remained undefeated: still standing. Other entertainers on the same program included Bill Cosby and Carmen McRae. Seeger did "Goodnight Irene," "Wimoweh!" and a satirical song about the quiz show scandals. Men in tuxedos and women in evening dresses, all clutching cocktails, listened attentively and appreciatively, even succumbing to Pete's charm and joining in on "Wimoweh!"

This busy period of Pete's existence, as he waited for his trial to come up, dovetailed with the early stages of what would become the 1960s folk boom. The Kingston Trio's version of the folk ballad "Tom Dooley" exploded onto the hit parade during the autumn of 1958, selling 2.8 million copies. Previously, in 1956, the Tarriers (featuring Erik Darling and Alan Arkin, the latter not yet a famous actor) charted in the top ten with the calypso-ish "Banana Boat Song." That same year, Harry Belafonte's debut album *Calypso* became a million-seller in both the United States and Britain.

The skiffle movement as well fed into the popularization of "folk" as a genre – good examples of this being Lonnie Donegan's 1956 hit version of "Rock Island Line" (with "John Henry" on the "B" side) and Nancy Whiskey's 1957 hit with her version of Elizabeth Cotten's "Freight Train." Out in California, a teenaged Joan Baez, after being brought as a thirteen year old to a 1954 Pete

Seeger concert in Palo Alto, bought herself a guitar and began working to master songs from his repertoire.

CHAPTER TEN:
BITTER BURLESQUE

Early in the morning of April 4th, 1961, Pete and Toshi Seeger bumped down their long driveway in Beacon, heading to New York City and Pete's sentencing for contempt of Congress. Two young filmmakers, brothers Michael and Philip Burton, sat in the backseat of the white Rambler Station wagon, their camera and sound equipment rolling. As Pete drove, Toshi waved back to their children, shouting goodbye and commenting to Pete that their eldest daughter, Mika – old enough to understand what was going on – seemed clearly quite nervous and upset.

As they headed south down Route 9D to the Bear Mountain Bridge, Pete practiced the prepared comments he would make in court when asked to speak before sentencing. Toshi held a little pad and read along with the script Pete had prepared. Once they got to the city, the couple pulled over and Toshi took the wheel for the trip across town. As they approached the neighborhood of the Foley Square courthouse, Pete plunked on his banjo and nervously rehearsed "Wasn't That A Time!" – this on the off-chance (unlikely, he knew) that the judge would agree to a request he planned to make: that he be permitted to sing the song the HUAC had thought so dangerous.

Pete's three-day (March 27 – 30) jury trial on 10 counts of contempt had been an exercise in frustration for both Pete and his attorney Paul Ross. "In his opening statement," reported the *Harvard Crimson*, "Seeger's attorney ... launched a wholesale attack on the Committee's unlimited investigating powers. He denied that the issue of the case was merely whether the folksinger had committed contempt by refusing to answer the questions as had been earlier suggested by the prosecutor, Irving Younger ... ."

Ross insisted Seeger's "rights under the first amendment were violated, and he had the right to say the questions were invalid. The investigation did not serve any valid legislative purpose. There was no question of national security involved, or of over-throwing the government by force or violence." Ross argued that "fundamental freedoms" were at stake. But in the end, Federal Judge Thomas F. Murphy agreed with Younger's assessment, stating that it was Seeger who was on trial, not the HUAC, and testimony would be strictly limited to the specific charges in question.

The government's primary witness, HUAC counsel Taverner – one of the two men who had questioned Seeger so vigorously in 1955 – insisted the HUAC investigations did in fact involve and inform legislative matters of the House of Representatives with regard to security against Communist threats. Since Seeger had been involved with various Communist-affiliated groups, it was completely legitimate for the Committee to probe into those affiliations with a view toward establishing, through the testimony of Seeger and others, a clear picture of the operation of these types of organizations, especially with regard to their outreach through celebrities.

Throughout the proceedings, especially in the case of witnesses called by the defense (including HUAC Committee Chairman Francis E. Walter) Judge Murphy repeatedly heard testimony first with the jury out of the room, in order to make sure questions and responses stuck to the facts of the contempt charge and did not – as was Ross's strategy – put on trial the legitimacy of the HUAC. Thus virtually none of Ross's points were demonstrated through testimony; and thus the trial's inevitable result: convictions on all ten counts – each related to a specific question to which Seeger had refused to respond in 1955.

Technically, the verdict was a sound one. Seeger had not answered the questions put to him by the Committee, and had not asserted the protection of the Fifth in doing so. The outcome of the trial was, in the end, no surprise to either Seeger or his attorney. Like countless practitioners of civil disobedience who had stood on their convictions in the past, Seeger had all along expected to be called to account for his conscientious stand – especially since Arthur Miller and others had already been found guilty in similar actions. The only question now was exactly what price would be paid.

Next morning, a headline in the *New York Post* said it all: DANGEROUS MINSTREL NABBED HERE. "Amid our larger tribulations," read the editorial, "the Justice Department has moved fearlessly and decisively against ballad singer Pete Seeger. ... That the combined powers of the House Committee and the Justice Department should be rallied to imprison him is a bitter burlesque. Some jail will be a more joyous place if he lands there, and things will be bleaker on the outside."

*

When one delves into the back-story of the trial, several fascinating facts come to light that have not, so far as I know, been commented upon in Seeger biographies to date. Shortly before he died in 1988, former Federal prosecutor Irving Younger wrote an extensive essay about his most interesting cases, this subsequently published in the *Minnesota Law Review*. In this document, the context and (in some ways startling) politics and personalities behind the trial stand revealed.

At the time of the Seeger prosecution, Younger was a 29-year-old recent appointee as Assistant U.S. Attorney for the Southern District of New York. He'd graduated from New York University Law School in 1958, and spent two years in private practice before joining the Justice Department under the newly-elected Kennedy administration. Younger was a thoughtful and keen

lawyer, a Democrat, and no fan of the HUAC.
Nevertheless, here he was prosecuting Seeger.

It had been a long time, six years, between Seeger's
1955 testimony and his eventual 1961 prosecution, and it
had been a full four years since his 1957 indictment. On the
surface, one might have expected the prosecution of Seeger
to proceed with full vigor under the relatively conservative
Republican Eisenhower administration, especially with
HUAC enthusiast Richard Nixon in office as vice
president. But this was not the case.

Early on, according to Younger, the Department of
Justice had pretty much ignored the Seeger case. "The
hysteria of the early 1950s … had crested. Whether the
Department of Justice would just as soon have proceeded
no further, perhaps dropping the case altogether after a
suitable number of years had gone by, I don't know. I do
know that the Seeger file had been relegated to the back of
a drawer in a storage cabinet in the United States
Attorney's office and that, as of the day I was sworn in,
nothing was happening in the case and nothing was
contemplated."

This was to change. "In January of 1961, leadership of
the Department of Justice shifted from William P. Rogers,
the Republican Attorney-General, to Robert F. Kennedy.
Before long, word went around the corridors of the United
States Attorney's office that the new Attorney-General
wanted the Seeger case pushed to a conclusion. The file
was retrieved from the back of its drawer and assigned to

me. My instructions were to ignore the whiskers on the case ... and try it."

At first glance, it seems surprising that Robert Kennedy would be pushing for Seeger's prosecution. At second glance, not so much. As a young attorney, Bobby Kennedy had been a ravenous bulldog investigator and interrogator [*aka*, counsel] for Joseph McCarthy's Permanent Subcommittee on Investigations, where he worked closely with Roy Cohn. RFK biographer Evan Thomas has speculated that McCarthyist anti-Communism appealed to Bobby's "black-and-white moralism." He thought the Senate Committee did good work, and the HUAC as well.

Kennedy remained personally loyal to McCarthy even after the Senator's censure. Per Thomas: "Disgraced by the Army-McCarthy hearings, the Wisconsin senator was fast becoming a pariah, which seemed to make Bobby fiercer in his defense. His football friends from Harvard recalled an angry blowup between [Kennedy aide] Ken O'Donnell and Bobby after the 1954 Harvard-Yale game. Perplexed at Bobby's stubborn refusal to recognize the shame of McCarthy, O'Donnell pleaded: 'What the hell is wrong with you?' In January 1955, CBS newsman Edward Murrow, whose exposé helped topple McCarthy, spoke at a banquet honoring the Junior Chamber of Commerce Ten Outstanding Young Men of 1954, one of whom, thanks to his father's finagling, was Bobby. Grim-faced, young Kennedy walked out during the speech."

It is perhaps worth noting and remembering here that the Kennedy administration, though painted largely liberal by friendly historians, had a definite conservative cast where it came to many issues. Frankly, the administration's various actions on civil rights were less initiatives than reactions to such pressures as the March on Washington, and were embarked upon quite cynically, at least given the tone within the Oval Office, where black writer and activist James Baldwin – a homosexual – was routinely referred to as "Martin Luther Queen" and where the decision was made to tap Martin Luther King Jr.'s telephones in order to learn more about the minister's alleged Communist ties. Against this backdrop, Younger proceeded with his unhappy mission, ably winning Seeger's conviction.

On the day of his sentencing, Seeger delivered his prepared remarks to the court:

> *After hearing myself talked about pro and con for three days, I am very grateful to say a few words, unrestricted words, myself.*
>
> *Firstly, I want to thank my lawyer deeply for his masterly preparation and presentation of my defense. He has worked over long weeks and months, and done all this knowing that it is beyond my power to pay him adequately for his work.*
>
> *I believe that he and great legal minds like Justice Hugo Black and Dr. Alexander Michaelson, and others,*

*have stated far better than I can the reasons that they
believe the First Amendment gives an American citizen
the right to refuse to speak upon certain occasions.*

*Secondly, I should like to state before this Court,
much as I did before Congressman Walter's Committee,
my conviction that I have never in my life said, or
supported, or sung anything in any way subversive of
my country. Congressman Walter stated that he was
investigating a conspiracy. I stated under oath that I had
never done anything conspiratorial. If he doubted my
word, why didn't he even question it? Why didn't he
have me indicted for perjury? Because, I believe, even he
knew that I was speaking the truth.*

*Some of my ancestors were religious dissenters who
came to America over 300 years ago. Others were
abolitionists in New England of the 1840s and 50s. I
believe that in choosing my present course I do no
dishonor to them, or to those who may come after me.*

*I am 42 years old, and count myself a very lucky
man. I have a wife and three healthy children, and we
live in a house we built with our own hands, on the
banks of the beautiful Hudson River. For twenty years I
have been singing folksongs of America and other lands
to people everywhere. I am proud that I never refused to
sing to any group of people because I might disagree
with some of the ideas of some of the people listening to
me. I have sung for rich and poor, for Americans of
every possible political and religious opinion and*

*persuasion, of every race, color, and creed. The House
Committee wished to pillory me because it didn't like
some few of the many thousands of places I have sung
for. Now it so happens that the specific song whose title
was mentioned in this trial "Wasn't That A Time!" is
one of my favorites. The song is apropos to this case. I
wonder if I might have your permission to sing it here
before I close?"*

[As expected, Judge Murphy refused
permission. Seeger, who had previously unpacked
his banjo, laid it down on the defense table.]

*Well, perhaps you will hear it some other time. A
good song can only do good, and I am proud of the songs
I have sung. I hope to be able to continue singing these
songs for all who want to listen, Republicans,
Democrats, and Independents. Do I have the right to
sing these songs? Do I have the right to sing them
anywhere?*

After the judge pronounced sentence (one year for
each of the ten counts, these to be served concurrently),
attorney Ross, client Seeger, and for that matter even
prosecutor Younger were surprised when Murphy refused
to grant bail pending appeal, and instead remanded Seeger
to custody. Younger recalled: "Seeger picked up his banjo
and handed it to his wife. With a marshal at either arm, he
was led away to the courthouse lock-up where he spent no

more than an hour in custody. His lawyers went from Judge Murphy's courtroom to the Court of Appeals [in the same building], which granted their application for bail pending appeal. Seeger had dinner at home that evening." Luckily, this was the only time Seeger would spend behind bars – although by Pete's recollection it was more like six hours than one. He got a free lunch, however, which he ate while listening to the chants of a large crowd gathered

outside the court building: "Free Pete! Free Pete!"

The day after his sentencing, Seeger took part in a folk concert at New York's Town Hall along with Grant Rogers, Bill McAdoo and several other performers. To thunderous applause, master-of-ceremonies Norman Studer, in introducing Pete, said "This voice of yours must not be silenced!" Rising with his banjo, Pete explained to the audience that he was "very nervous" and asked for their help in singing "This Land is Your Land."

Backstage, concert goers approached Pete again and again, expressing support and clutching the newsletter "For Pete's Sake" – one of Harold's ideas for raising money to pay for the defense – which Seeger autographed. Later on, Seeger emerged from the stage door to the sound of a large crowd outside chanting "We want Pete! We want

Pete!" Raising his hand for quiet, a smiling Seeger shouted: "I love you all." Then, kidding: "But don't go making such a scene. They [the authorities] will yell 'riot!'"

Three weeks later, on April 29th, Seeger's old Almanac friend Cisco Houston died of lung cancer out in San Bernadino, California. The following evening, April 30th, Seeger played to a packed house at New York's Village Gate. The audience included a frail, chain-smoking Woody Guthrie, sprung from his hospital room for the occasion. Seeger dedicated the first song to Cisco. The evening's proceedings were recorded by Columbia Records for what was to be Seeger's first release on the label. (More on Seeger and Columbia very shortly.)

Almost exactly one year after Seeger's sentencing – April 9th, 1962 – Paul Ross and another attorney, Samual M. Koenigsberg (who specialized in appellate work), argued Seeger's appeal. No longer was Seeger on trial. Now what was on trial were the court proceedings. Six weeks after oral arguments, the Court of Appeals reversed Seeger's conviction, but did so on a mere technicality: that the original indictment had failed to explicitly define the legislative source of the authority for the sub-committee of the HUAC before which Seeger had refused to answer. That same week, the Kingston Trio's rendition of "Where Have All the Flowers Gone?" entered the top forty charts.

"That ended the Seeger case," notes Younger, "and I wasn't disappointed. My sympathies lay with Seeger. If I had been on the Court of Appeals, I would have voted with the other judges to reverse the conviction, but I would have urged them to write a different sort of opinion. In the Seeger case, the Court of Appeals neither condemned the Un-American Activities Committee nor acknowledged a witness's right to refuse to answer questions about the witness's political beliefs and activities. The Court based its reversal on a technical ground, a ground smacking of pettifoggery. Had the Court chosen to write a more forthright opinion, it would have said that the Committee's investigation and Seeger's indictment were phenomena peculiar to the McCarthy days, that those days had come to an end, and that the Court was not going to contribute to their revival even by so little as an affirmance of this conviction." (Note: Arthur Miller's 1957 conviction on the same charges had been overturned in 1958, but also on a technicality and not in a manner that in any way questioned the fundamental authority of the HUAC or affirmed the First Amendment argument.)

Two months after Seeger's successful appeal, Irving Younger stood on a Fire Island beach with an old friend. "How could you," the friend asked, "prosecute Pete Seeger for doing what the Constitution gives him a right to do?" In response, Younger gave his friend a crash course in the ethics of the law. Younger explained how, as an officer of the court, "a lawyer's moral sense requires of him nothing else but vigorous advocacy, without regard to the moral quality of the client or the cause. ... The lawyer's commitment is embodied in no single document, but inheres in the lawyer's obligation to give any client and any cause his advocacy, regardless of his own moral judgment, because the question whether the client or the cause deserves a hearing is too profound for men to answer."

In Younger's view, the court system of American justice only worked if there was steadfast, informed and impassioned advocacy on both sides of every case. The lawyer's ultimate duty was to the process and procedures of trial, out of which truth would, hopefully, emerge. Digesting this, Younger's old friend of many years responded: "It doesn't make sense to me and I don't understand it. The fact is you're the guy who prosecuted Pete Seeger. That's a guy I don't want to know. This friendship is over." To this anecdote, recorded 26 years after the conversation, Younger adds just one line: "I haven't seen him since that day."

The rationale above is probably what Younger was referring to when, many years after the case, he bumped into Toshi and Pete Seeger at a social event. "I wasn't doing anything wrong," Younger volunteered. "I'd be willing to prosecute you again."

CHAPTER ELEVEN:
JOE STALIN'S BLUES

John Hammond was about as big a name as the recording industry could boast during the 1950s and 60s. An eastern aristocrat loaded with Vanderbilt blood and Vanderbilt money, he'd dropped out of Yale in 1931 in order to pursue a career in the music field – first as a reviewer and later as a talent scout and record producer. The young jazz aficionado developed close relationships with Benny Goodman (whose band he helped finance) and Fletcher Henderson among others.

Hammond was instrumental – no pun intended – in getting white band leaders to bring black virtuosos (such as Henderson) into their organizations, and vice versa. In 1938 he organized the now-legendary "Spirituals to Swing" concert at New York's Carnegie Hall, featuring artists whose music had never before been recognized by presentation in such a prestigious venue: Sonny Terry, Big Bill Broonzy, Ida Cox, Big Joe Turner, Sister Rosetta Tharpe and others. In a long career with Columbia Records – during which he produced a range of jazz and eventually folk and rock artists – Hammond amassed an amazing track record of discovering and promoting not only superb but truly seminal musicians ranging from Billie Holiday and Aretha Franklin to (eventually) Leonard Cohen, Stevie Ray Vaughn and Bruce Springsteen.

Hammond had been a supporter of People's Artists back in the day, and was active in the civil rights movement. In 1961, while Seeger still stood convicted, Hammond developed a conviction of his own that the folksinger belonged on the Columbia label. It seems his clout was big enough to overcome, at least partially, a still very powerful corporate bias against the musician. Hammond took his proposal to Columbia Records president Goddard Lieberson, who in turn – given Seeger's controversial profile – called Columbia Senior VP Richard Salant to test the waters. According to Hammond, who listened in on the speaker-phone conversation, Salant responded: "We don't need him, and he's not welcome on CBS Television." But then Salant asked Lieberson if he thought Seeger would "sell," to which Lieberson replied: "I wouldn't be calling you if I didn't." In that case, business was business. Salant gave the green light for Lieberson and Hammond to proceed. (Hammond would soon also sign Bob Dylan, after Seeger brought the young singer to his attention.) Seeger was to spend more than a decade with the label, but it would be years before he'd make it on to CBS Television – or, for that matter, *any* television network.

When the ABC program *Hootenanny* (launched 1963) refused to book Seeger, *Village Voice* columnist and free speech advocate Nat Hentoff rushed into print with the story. "That Ole McCarthy Hoot!" ran the headline. "*Hootenanny*, a weekly folk music series, starts on the

American Broadcasting Company on April 6. In the
current issue of *Broadside* (east coast edition), the charge is
made that Pete Seeger has been blacklisted by the new
program." *Broadside* also reported Joan Baez had refused to
appear on the show unless Seeger was given a booking.
"I've checked the story with several sources, and it is true,"
wrote Hentoff. The same went for Pete's old group, the
Weavers – this by order of some unnamed "Kafaesque
judge" at the network.

"The term 'hootenanny,' ..." Hentoff continued, "was
first popularized in its present context by Pete Seeger and
Woody Guthrie. (The irony of Pete's exclusion is similar to
those years when Charlie Parker was banned from
Birdland.)" Hentoff went on to point out that four months
earlier, Seeger and the Weavers, after an initial booking,
had been dis-invited from a CBS program (sponsored,
ironically, by the Anti-Defamation League of B'nai B'rth)
entitled "Dinner with the President," meant to celebrate
the 50th anniversary of the League, and featuring an award
presentation to JFK.

Hentoff challenged other folksingers to follow Baez's
example and boycott *Hootenanny*. Tom Paxton, Mary
Travers, Bob Dylan and others answered the call by
forming a *Hootenanny* Boycott Committee. Others decided
to appear on the program – but with good reason. Pete had
asked them to. Judy Collins recalls Harold Leventhal, Pete
and Jac Holzman (founder of the Elektra and Nonesuch
record labels) calling a meeting of performers at Harold's

office to discuss the situation. "Harold had, of course, managed Pete since the early Weavers days,"says Judy. "He had stood by Seeger in every confrontation Pete had faced with HUAC. He knew what they were up against." As Judy remembers the meeting, Harold expressed the view that the boycott was probably, in the grand scheme of things, a bad idea. *Hootenanny* represented a great step forward for the popularization of folk music (and topical music, which the program in fact welcomed), and should be embraced despite the despicable blacklisting of Pete.

"Then Pete … stood up to speak, and told those of us gathered that afternoon that *not* doing the show would hurt the entire folk movement. Pete said the same thing to everyone who was torn about appearing on *Hootenanny*." Not long after, Pete even filled in at last minute for a scheduled performance of the Tarriers at the Village Gate when a short-notice offer for a *Hootenanny* appearance conflicted with their Village Gate gig. In the end, over the course of two years, artists ranging from Collins to the Clancy Brothers appeared on the show, all with Pete's blessing. A few, however – Baez and Dylan among them, along with Tommy Makem who let the Clancys go on without him – still chose to stay away. At one point *Hootenanny* invited Pete to perform with the condition that he first sign a loyalty oath. As the network probably expected (and hoped), Seeger refused.

Partially in response to the *Hootenanny* debacle, and on the heels of a 1963-64 world tour (during which he'd been a featured guest on French, British, German, Norwegian, Japanese and Australian television, as well on programs in a host of other countries), Seeger launched his own small television enterprise. Independently produced, *Rainbow Quest* aired on a UHF station (WNJU – 47) in metropolitan New York and eventually on six other similarly small stations across the nation.

The format, as one might expect, was anti-glitz, anti-commercial and anti-overproduction. A small table and a few chairs and benches made up the "set." Programs were videotaped in black and white, with only two cameras, one of them usually "manned" by Toshi. Friends such as Judy Collins, Tom Paxton, Tommy Makem and the Clancys, Donovan, Rev. Gary Davis, Richard and Mimi Fariña, Elizabeth Cotten, Ralph Stanley, Doc Watson and Johnny and June Carter Cash stopped by to play and chat – for free. There was no studio audience, no applause, and no plugging of one's latest record. The program ran 52 minutes, usually with two or three guests per show. In all, Toshi and Pete produced 39 episodes during the years 1965-66 before they ran out of money to sustain the program, which had constantly run in the red and which they'd supported with their own personal funds. (Through 1967/68, New York's PBS station WNDT – 13 [now WNET] reran *Rainbow Quest* to a far wider audience.)

During the summer of 1967, longtime Seeger fans Tommy and Dick Smothers, empowered by high ratings for their CBS "Smothers Brothers Comedy Hour," arranged for the network to allow Pete onto their program. During the taping, Pete performed "Wimoweh!" and several other numbers, including the title track from his most recent Columbia release: "Waist Deep in the Big Muddy." The song, penned by Seeger, voiced a fervent protest against American involvement in Vietnam, and contained a thinly-veiled attack on President Lyndon Johnson, the "big fool" who "says to push on." Seeger's intention to perform the song on CBS gained significant press attention, and drew a record audience to the broadcast of September 10th – but at the last minute network censors cut the number. The result was a firestorm of criticism aimed at CBS. "Is the presidency so teetery that it cannot withstand the musical barbs of a folksinger?" asked one editorial. "And is our democracy so fragile that songs of social protest must be stricken from the public airwaves? We think not." Eventually, public pressure forced CBS to relent. Seeger performed the song on a Smothers program the following February.

Two years later, a newly-bearded Seeger guested on another network program, the ABC production hosted by his friend Johnny Cash. The country legend had endeavored to invite Seeger on one year earlier, in his first season, but was rebuffed by network executives. When negotiating for his second season after the show became a ratings hit, an empowered Cash made it a part of the deal that Seeger (or anyone else Cash felt like inviting) would be welcome, no questions asked. His first call was to

Seeger. Appearing on the show (taped at Nashville's legendary Ryman Auditorium, home to the Grand Ole Opry), Seeger performed several numbers, none of them particularly controversial, except that in a duet with Cash on "Worried Man Blues" he added a bit of mild political commentary. Harold had advised Pete to "go easy" on the Cash show lest other potential bookers get the idea that *every* attempt to broadcast him was going to lead to controversy and attendant hassles. Backstage during rehearsals, Cash confided to Pete that there had been a wave of right wing protest and hate mail following Cash's announcement that he'd be hosting Seeger on the program. To anyone who asked, Cash explained Seeger was one of the finest Americans he had ever had the privilege to know. Cash made no apologies. He was proud to stand by Seeger's side.

In August of 1972, two years after the Cash performance, Seeger joined Arlo Guthrie on NBC's "Tonight Show" hosted by Johnny Carson. Seeger shared the couch with Joey Bishop, Marty Feldman and "Hee-Haw" bombshell Sherry Miles. Evidently not censored at all this time out, he performed his latest, most strident anti-Vietnam War song yet, "Last Train to Nuremberg." Comparing the crimes of the United States in Vietnam to the crimes of the Nazis, "Last Train to Nuremberg" made "Big Muddy" sound like a lullaby. There was no push-back.

*

Near the end of July 1959, Lillian Hellman hosted a
house-party in Seeger's honor following a concert in
Provincetown, on Cape Cod. The talk turned to sailing,
which Seeger had never done. "Up until that time sailing
to me was something rich people did on yachts." The next
morning, a young friend of Hellman's took the folksinger
out for his first little voyage. Catching the bug, Seeger soon
bought himself a tiny used boat and began spending days
out on the murky, polluted waters of the Hudson.

He not only enjoyed the sport, but (as was his habit
with most things) soon derived an important metaphorical
theme from the exercise. As all sailors know, it is actually
possible to make decided progress sailing *against the wind.*
This is a simple art: deploying strategic port and starboard
tacks to take the force blowing against you and transform
it into a force to help you advance forward. "I think of Dr.
King, who zig-zagged his way along. They'd throw him in
jail one place, and he'd get support. He'd zig another place
and get more support and more press." In his own
personal experience, Seeger must have thought of all those
protests helping publicize his performances, raising
awareness of free speech at risk, and selling tickets.

Soon he also came to view the polluted Hudson River
as a metaphor. If such a broken and decimated thing as the
sewage- and chemical-choked river could be resurrected,
then what else might be possible in a broken and
decimated world? The efforts of Seeger and many other
Hudson Valley residents to build and develop the

programs of the *Clearwater* – "America's Environmental Flagship", a working replica of the traditional Hudson River sloops which once dominated Hudson River trade – have been well-documented. Seeger played a critical role in the fundraising, during which he was attacked by many members of the left for accepting a large donation from DeWitt and Lila Wallace, the ultra-conservative co-founders of *Readers Digest*.

Today, after nearly fifty years, the sloop still sails. And the Hudson is partially restored, even though polychlorinated biphenyls (courtesy of General Electric) make native upriver fish unsafe to eat, even though an antiquated nuclear reactor sits on a geologic fault line at Indian Point (Peekskill), even though potential hydrofracking threatens the Hudson watershed, and even though many industrial discharges continue as before. But so it goes. Late in life, Seeger was not surprised. He knew not all good things were possible; but he also knew all good things should be striven for. Little victories were still victories.

The legacy of red-baiting followed Seeger into the realm of environmentalism. During a 1970 *Clearwater* waterfront event at Cold Spring (within three miles of the Seeger home), right-wingers interrupted an evening concert by the Hudson Valley Philharmonic. The night before, the *Clearwater* crew had been forced to leave the pier and anchor off-shore after stones were thrown at the vessel from out of the darkness.

On the evening of the event, following a beautiful performance of Handel's "Water Music," the conductor called Seeger to the stage to describe *Clearwater's* programs and make a pitch for contributions. As soon as he started speaking, "a large flag-waving group appeared … marching across the pier and through the assembled audience." They carried a twenty-foot banner: "Clean Up the Hudson. Get rid of Pollution Pete." As scholar Joseph Janeti reports: "Threats were hurled, and at the moment that it seemed violence was about to break out, the orchestra struck up 'The Star-Spangled Banner.' The demonstrators were momentarily stalled. Not sure whether to salute their anthem or storm the stage and kill the 'commies,' they applauded and booed at the same time. Some waved flags, others fists. The confusion went on just long enough to allow the local, state and county police to surround the mob and stave off violence. Some of the more belligerent demonstrators had to be carried off." Cold Spring police escorted Seeger to his car and made sure he got safely out of the parking lot. Before he left, a demonstrator shouted at him: "Just tell me

if you're a Communist!" Seeger responded calmly: "I'm about as much a Communist as the American Indian."

*

Rhetorically, Pete didn't do himself any favors when, in this and other debates, and also in print, he repeatedly compared his vision of Communism to that – if we can even call it that – practiced by many Native American tribes in centuries past. At worst, the analogy sounded like a purposeful white-washing and misdirection; at best, it sounded like the ultimate in naivete. The fundamental share-and-share-alike practice that had existed in many tribal cultures in no way resembled strict, top-down, planned economies such as Marx had envisioned.

The Native Americans' neighbor-to-neighbor generosity was *liaise-faire* rather than doctrinaire, and based on foundations of custom and spirituality. It was not imposed by authority, but rather tradition. What is more, it was not even an economy *per se*, in the modern sense (the sense Marx put on the word *economy*), being based for the most part on hunting and gathering. But Seeger's musings did not arise from an intention to white-wash, nor from naivete, nor from a desire to confuse the issue. Rather, what he endeavored (somewhat unsuccessfully) to express was an idealized vision. Though the ideal would most certainly never be reached, it remained of value and relevance as an ethical star to steer towards.

Describing himself as "more conservative than
Goldwater," Seeger would make the point that Goldwater
"just wanted to turn the clock back to when there was no
income tax. I want to turn the clock back to when people
lived in small villages and took care of each other." In the
same 1995 *New York Times* interview where he made his
Goldwater comment, Seeger said: "I still call myself a
Communist, because Communism is no more what Russia
made of it than Christianity is what the churches make of
it. But if by some freak of history Communism had caught
up with this country, I would have been one of the first
people thrown in jail. As my father used to say: 'The truth
is a rabbit in a bramble patch. All you can do is circle
around and say it's somewhere in there.'" Stalin, he added,
had been "a supremely cruel misleader." (This was a point
Seeger had made more than once before, including in his
1993 autobiography *Where Have All the Flowers Gone? - A
Singer's Stories, Songs, Seeds, Robberies.*) Speaking to
Washington Post reporter Michael Hill in 2007, Seeger sang
him a recent song - "Joe Stalin's Blues" - in which he
condemned the dictator and his atrocities. Hill called the
song "as scathing as any tune in the folk legend's long
career."

Seeger's "Communism" was his own unique variation
on the theme, in no way resembling anything Stalin or any
other red tyrant would recognize as doctrine, and in no
way resembling what the man or woman on the street
thought of whenever he or she heard the ominous word.

(One recalls Irwin Silber's remark from 1946, already quoted previously, that Seeger's "basis in Marxism was [too] sketchy" to make him in any way an effective party functionary. Some things never change.)

The subtlety in Seeger's rhetoric almost always got lost in the translation. Subtleties don't travel very well in our sound-bite culture. The one simple and constantly misunderstood phrase most people heard and remembered was: "I still call myself a Communist."

EPILOGUE

My friend Pete Seeger died on January 27th, 2014, while I was in the midst of writing this book. His wife Toshi had passed the previous July, and I'd last seen Pete in Manhattan in October at a memorial gathering for Toshi. At the time he seemed frail and quite suddenly – which sounds ridiculous to say when one is referencing a 94 year old – aged.

I'd previously been with him not long before Toshi's passing, when he and I (and a few of our fellow wooden boat enthusiasts) paid a visit to the International Yacht Restoration School in Newport, RI, not far from where I live. At the time, he seemed quite spry and quite sharp. He bounded up some forty steep steps to peer down into the bowels of an ancient schooner in the early stages of a rebuild, and was full of detailed questions for the shipwrights. Out in the parking lot, surveying the many eco bumper-stickers on the back of my truck, he wryly commented: "Ed, you must be one of those environmental wackos I've been hearing so much about. Shame on you." But at Toshi's invitation-only memorial tribute he moved slowly and unsteadily, spoke haltingly, and made many slips, such as introducing musician Guy Davis as the "daughter" of his old friends Ossie Davis and Ruby Dee. He was clearly losing ground.

So I was not surprised to hear he'd passed. (It was a phone call in the wee hours of the morning, a call timed to wake us before we woke ourselves, lest my wife and I hear the news via less personal means: social media or television.) Neither was I surprised by the outpouring of memorials and tributes on television, in newspapers and magazines, and elsewhere. I was gratified to hear of Bruce Springsteen, on tour in the Southern Hemisphere, stopping in the midst of a concert in Cape Town to acknowledge Pete's passing, and to note President Obama's official condolences published by the White House. The tributes from other musicians and politicians and just plain folks were too numerous to count. My own personal Facebook wall filled up with comments and condolences from people who'd known what Pete meant to me. A talk program on the Grateful Dead's Serius Satellite station asked me on to speak about Pete's legacy and his profound influence on the music of the 1960s, including Jerry Garcia and Bobby Weir and the other boys.

I was, sadly, also not surprised when the intellectual (I use the term loosely) heirs of the previous generation's red-baiters seized on Seeger's passing as an excuse to excoriate him one last time. Writing in *National Review,* John Fund called Seeger a "totalitarian troubadour" and "Communism's pied piper." In the same publication, Howard Husock brooded on the insidiously Machiavellian way in which Seeger ("America's most successful Communist") had "claimed folk music for the left."

Husock sees the anti-war anthem "Where Have All
the Flowers Gone?" as a reaction to "McCarthy-era
pressure" which demanded of Seeger and other political
songsmiths that they come up with a new and more
"subtle" form of political messaging than that which had
previously defined their music. Husock sees as sinister all
songs which speak to
peace generally as a
concept, or brotherhood
generally as a concept,
as opposed to
confronting specific
political arguments and
movements head-on. In
other words, to Husock's
mind, the belligerent
"Times They Are
A'Changin'" is a far
more honest and less
insidious thing than the
mournful, popular
"Abraham, Martin and
John," which plays on
the emotions of an easily-duped public in order to
surreptitiously spread vile leftist sentiment.

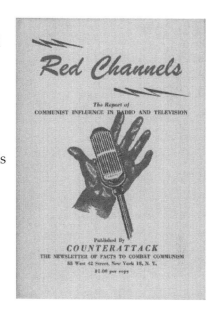

Husock goes on to take Seeger to task for co-opting
Ecclesiastes in "Turn! Turn! Turn!" and slipping in a line or
two suggesting peace is generally a better condition than

war. Husock also dislikes "If I Had a Hammer" – with its suggestion that if so armed the singer would "hammer out love between my brothers and my sisters." Love between brothers and sisters is obviously code for Communist rebellion, just as the contemporary Tea Party's references to "inner city populations" is code for blacks. But it is the popular success of this music that Husock finds most alarming, and that he is sure Seeger had in mind from the start as he worked to deploy flawless and catchy musical craftsmanship in the service of the enemy. And to think the Kingston Trio never caught on to how they were being used to radicalize and corrupt American youth. It appears Seeger was Ho Chi Min's Burt Bacharach. (Or perhaps Bacharach was, given his "What the World Needs Now" - you know: "love sweet love" and all that.)

Citing a completely unsourced "estimate" appearing on a dubious web site called "The Richest," University of Georgia associate professor Stephen Mihm has tagged Pete as a man worth $4.2 million at the time of his death, and implied that his working class hero, tattered-work-shirt persona was in large measure a fraud. (Evidently Stalinism pays well. I'm sure Pete's children and grandchildren will be delighted, and astonished, to learn about the windfall they are about to harvest.) Michael Moynihan, cultural news editor of *The Daily Beast*, writes that Seeger, "once an avowed Stalinist, was a political singer devoted to a sinister political system – a position he held long after the Soviet experiment drenched itself in blood and collapsed

in ignominy." (I'm still searching for a direct quote from
Seeger in which he says the Soviet Union is just peachy.
Perhaps one day I'll come across something. I notice none
of his right-wing critics seem to have found one either.)

In *The American Spectator*, Mark Tooley (President of
the Institute on Religion and Democracy) condemns Seeger
for having protested against the American government's
preferred dictators, whom he evidently did not realize
were nicer guys than Stalin. "Seeger [sang] against the
oppressions of rightest dictators like Chile's Augusto
Pinochet without apparently understanding that such
authoritarian tyrants lacked the cosmic ambitions of
messianic totalitarians like Stalin. … Authoritarians jailed
and killed their political opponents. Totalitarians
demanded total worship of themselves and/or their
ideology." And the difference is? (By the way, before
starting with the Institute of Religion and Democracy,
Tooley was in the CIA.)

Then we have Ron Radosh, a one-time banjo student
of Pete's and reformed Red-Diaper Baby who has an ax to
grind with the culture in which he was raised: "Seeger's
voice was heard in defense of causes in which only fools
could still believe." (I'm just going to leave that one alone.
It speaks for itself.) Always accurate, Radosh goes on to
report that Pete's cabin on the mountainside was "built
from scrap." Looked like logs to me. But what do I know?

An old political cartoon from the 1950s shows two
HUAC inquisitors standing over a man who is bound and

gagged in a chair. The inquisitors say to him: "All we want is the truth as we know it." Stalinism in action.

Seeger's entire fight – the one for which he willingly put himself at risk of prison, the one he could have quite easily avoided (while still preserving both his dignity and his honor) by simply taking the Fifth Amendment – was about *free speech*. By this I mean free speech as a concept taken *entire* – not just in the United States, but everywhere. His bravery, uprightness, honesty and patriotism in this battle needs no apology.

Just like civil rights and the protesting of ridiculous and unconscionable wars such as were fought in Vietnam and Iraq, and just like working to save our endangered environment, such a thing as free speech is *not* a cause in which only fools can believe.

- EJR
Wickford, RI
March 29th, 2014

NOTES

Chapter One – Seeger's Slave Gangs
"Seeger's slave gangs ... " Malone, Bill C. *Music From the True Vine: Mike Seeger's Life and Musical Journey.* (Raleigh: University of North Carolina Press, 2011). 43.

Chapter Two – Double-Edged Sword
"when the Committee was finally brought into being ... " Wills, Garry. "Introduction" to *Scoundrel Time* by Lillian Hellman (Boston: Little, Brown & Co., 1976). 19-20.

"looked on powerlessly ... " "The Spy Who Made McCarthy." *Guardian.* 26 January 1999.

"Dickstein ran a lucrative trade ... " Browning, Lynnley (*Globe* Staff). "Spy vs. Spy vs. Spy." *Boston Globe.* 14 February 1999.

Chapter Three – Fellow Travelers
"thousands who continually ... " Chambers, Whittaker. *Witness* (Chicago, Regnery Books, 1985). 12.

"dedicated revolutionists ... " *Witness.* 33.

"slowly, reluctantly ... " *Witness.* 15.

"For the right to tie itself ... " Kimmage, Michael. *The Conservative Turn: Whittaker Chambers, Lionel Trilling, and the Lessons of Anti-Communism* (Cambridge, Harvard University Press, 2009). 233.

"a coterie of professional musicians ... " Pescatello, Ann M. *Charles Seeger: A Life in American Music* (Pittsburgh: University of Pittsburgh Press, 1991). 109 – 12.

"There is no reason why ... " *Charles Seeger: A Life in American Music.* 116.

"It was quite different from ... " Dunaway, David King. *How Can I Keep From Singing?* (New York: McGraw Hill, 1981). 41.

"These recordings are distributed ... " Friedrich, Carl. "The Poison in Our System." *Atlantic Monthly*, June 1940, Volume 167, No. 6. 668.

"Only lefties are going to hear it ... " Kaufman, Will. *Woody Guthrie: American Rebel* (Urbana: University of Illinois Press, 2011). 70.

"If there were six more teams ... " Cohen, Ronald D. *Rainbow Quest: The Folk Music Revival and American Society, 1940-1970* (Amherst: University of Massachusetts Press, 2002). 29.

"Our whole politics ... " Willens, Doris. *Lonesome Traveler: The Life of Lee Hays* (Lincoln: The University of Nebraska Press, 1993). 69.

"not from their own desire ... " *How Can I Keep from Singing?* 87-8.

Chapter Four – Sentimentalists
"sentimentalist ... " *Witness.* 253.

"exalted in his new identity … " Tanenhaus, Sam. *Whittaker Chambers: A Biography*. (New York: Random House, 1997). 87.

"Make a singing labor movement … " *How Can I Keep from Singing?* 117.

"Because of his independence … " Ibid. 118.

"basis in Marxism … " Ibid. 130.

Chapter Five – Songs and Stones

"We knew we were beginning … " *Lonesome Traveler*. 93.

"CIO unions would purge … " Ibid. 93.

"play folksongs … " *How Can I Keep from Singing?* 124.

"in the next two years … " Ibid. 125.

"asked me if it was true … " *Scoundrel Time*. 121.

"at which Pete Seeger played banjo … " Kirkpatrick, Jeane J. *Legitimacy and Force: Political and Moral Dimensions* (New Brunswick: Transaction Press, 1988). 468.

"I should have left much earlier … " Wilkinson, Alec. *The Protest Singer: An Intimate Portrait of Pete Seeger* (New York: Random House, 2009). 116.

"The Peekskill Riots demonstrate … " Scott Linford's review of Will Kaufman's *Woody Guthrie: American Radical* (*Ethnomusicology Review*, Volume 16, 2011).

"In Russia I felt … " Paul Robeson testimony before the HUAC, 12 June 1956.

"all Africa remembers … " Philip S. Foner. *Paul Robeson Speaks*. (New York: Citadel Press, 1978). 238.

Chapter Six – America Singing

"at the efforts of Communists ... " *How Can I Keep from Singing?* 134.

"When I hear America singing ... " Winkler, Allan M. *To Everything There is a Season: Pete Seeger and the Power of Song* (New York: Oxford University Press, 2009). 61.

"Red-tinged ... " *Time* Magazine, 25 September 1950.

Chapter Seven – A Light Burning Low

"the extravagance of human tenderness ... " James, William. *The Varieties of Religious Experience* (Rockville, MD: Arc Manor, 2008). 263. Further James quotes from same page.

"tried to stay hungry ... " *Lonesome Traveler: The Life of Lee Hays*. 194.

"Prestige is overrated ... " Seeger, Pete. "Pete Seeger Talks to Teens." *Seventeen* Magazine. November 1963.

"Swedenborgian ... " Seeger's explanation of his faith was made to the Rev. Richard S. Parker, at that time Superintendent of the Long Island West District of the United Methodist Church, who described it in a conversation with the author not long after. Parker had previously been minister at a Methodist Church in Poughkeepsie, NY, during which period he and his wife Grace developed a close friendship with Toshi and Pete Seeger.

"Pete's daughter, who was about my age ... "
Guardian Music Blog. 28 January 2014.

Chapter Eight – The Last Free Place in America
"outdated ... " *Whittaker Chambers: A Biography.* 284.
"American Communists [were] as dangerous ... "
Mailer, Norman. *Oswald's Tale: An American Mystery* (New York: Random House, 1995). 422.
"because he felt it was ... " *How Can I Keep from Singing?* 191.
"I cannot and will not ... " *Scoundrel Time.* 93.
"I am not going to answer ... " The complete text of Seeger's testimony is widely available on the Web.
"Harold Leventhal told Pete ... " *Lonesome Traveler: The Life of Lee Hays.* 164.
"I had many twinges of conscience ... " Ibid. 166.
"You don't have to worry about me ... " Cray, Ed. *Ramblin' Man: The Life and Times of Woody Guthrie* (New York: W.W. Norton, 2004). 378.
Ibid. 372.

Chapter Nine – Purgatory
"The first time I ever got involved in anything ... "
Guthrie, Arlo. "Arlo Guthrie Remembers Pete Seeger." *Billboard.* 31 January 2014.
"Morman Tabernacle Campfire ... " Corliss, Richard. "Why Pete Seeger Mattered." *Time* Magazine. 28 January 2014.

"Seeger had this amazing ability ... " Bob Dylan interview from PBS "American Masters" documentary *Pete Seeger: The Power of Song*. 2008.

Chapter Ten – Bitter Burlesque
"Two young filmmakers ..." Details here, and about the Town Hall Concert on April 5th, 1961 ["This voice of yours ..."] come directly from the film "Wasn't That a Time!" by Michael and Philip Burton. 1961.

"Seeger's attorney ..." Churchill, Michael. "Seeger Defense Attacks HUAC at Trial Opening." *Harvard Crimson*. 28 March 1961.

"DANGEROUS MINSTREL NABBED HERE." *New York Post*. 31 March 1961.

"The hysteria of the early 1950s ..." Younger, Irving. "Autobiography – Prosecuting." *Minnesota Law Review*. April 1989. All subsequent Younger quotes from this document.

"black-and-white moralism ..." Thomas, Evan. *Robert Kennedy: His Life* (New York: Simon & Schuster, 2000). 65.

" Disgraced by the Army-McCarthy hearings ..." Ibid. 67.

"After hearing myself talked about ..." Seeger, Pete. *The Incompleat Folksinger* (New York: Simon & Schuster, 1972). 470-471.

"Almost exactly one year later ..." For details on the appeal arguments and decision see *The Federal Reporter, Second Series*, Volume 303, page 480.

"I wasn't doing anything wrong ..." *How Can I Keep from Singing?* 308.

Chapter 11 – Joe Stalin's Blues

"We don't need him ..." Hammond, John and Irving Townsend. *John Hammond On Record: An Autobiography* (New York: Ridge Press, 1977). 346.

"That Ole McCarthy Hoot!" Hentoff, Nat. *The Village Voice*. 14 March 1963.

"Harold had, of course, managed Pete ..." Collins, Judy. *Sweet Judy Blue Eyes: My Life in Music* (New York: Three Rivers Press, 2011). 150-151.

"Is the presidency so teetery ..." *How Can I Keep from Singing?* 264.

"Up until that time ..." Hoekstra, David. "Pete Seeger and the Sound of America." *Chicago Sun Times*. 28 January 2014.

"a large flag-waving group ..." Janeti, Joseph. *Experiment in Social Change: One View of the First Five Years of the Hudson River Sloop CLEARWATER*. Ph.D. Dissertation. Department of English/American Studies. University of Michigan. 1975.

"more conservative than Goldwater ..." *New York Times*. 21 January 1995.

"as scathing as any song ..." Hill, Michael. "Pete Seegers Sings Out Against Stalin." *Washington Post*. 31 August 2007.

Epilogue
"totalitarian troubadour ... " Fund, John. "Totalitarian Troubadour." *National Review* Online. 28 January 2014.

"America's most successful Communist ... " Husock, Howard. "Pete Seeger: Cultural Warrior Extraordinaire." *National Review* Online. 28 January 2014.

"once an avowed Stalinist ... " Moynihan, Michael. "The Death of Stalin's Songbird." *The Daily Beast*. 29 January 2014.

"Seeger sang against ... " Tooley, Mark. "Pete Seeger, Stalin and God." *The American Spectator*. 31 January 2014.

"Seeger's voice was heard ... " Radosh, Ron. "The Red Warbler." *The Weekly Standard*. 10 February 2014.

ACKNOWLEDGMENTS

I am indebted to many people who helped bring this book to fruition, most especially: Jeanne Salvesen Phillips, Melanie Salvesen Jackson, Rik Palieri, George Mann, LeeAnne Geenen, Lee Baldwin, Elaine Ricci, Rickie Peterson, Shaun Tinsley, Ian Carr, Ramsay Leimenstoll, Douglas Arnold, Annie Karam, Raines Cohen, Eleanor Walden, Sheri Solomon, Mark Fisher, Mary Katherine Aldin, Kenneth Giles, Jeff Pudlo, The Banjo Project, Leapfrog Press, Mike Tassone, Matt Mulany-Green, Mary B. and John Hall, Paul Gross, Richard Ilomaki, John Bloomberg-Rissman, Elliott Battzedek, Tom Score, John Perry Barlow, Robin Jones, Jeremy Kerr, Kevin Cole, Vernon Owens, Jean-Pierre Devin, Faye Lynch, Walt Burnham, Jeff Bernstein, Dennis Cox, Benjamin Slaughter, Monte Rogneby, Deb Hiett, Gigi Fris, Rick Ritter, Denise Costello, Ann Bingley Gallops, Ency Austin, Murphy Romano, Billy Bragg, Joe Reilly, Gerhard Randers-Pehrson, Jim McGuinn, Elaine M. Meade, Leda Shapiro, Melissa Frieze Karolak, Bob Weir, Teri Noris, Susan Reid Bozso, Barry Ollman, David Elisila, Happy Traum, Sarah Taft, Erika Hamerquist, Lawrence Wallin, Allen Josephs, Susan Follett, Pat Lown, Robert Kunkel, Judi Zdziera, Carl Allen, Arthur Burns, Marie Kutch, Timothy Len East, Mark Smith, Moira Cameron, Carolyn Moon, Michael Slik, Tommy Lee Stoner, Doug Lowe, Paull Robathan, Daniel

Rosen, Marc Jeffrey Mikulich, Veva Silva, Eric Liberman, Jimmy Capuano, Chuck Ananda, Warren Senders, Meg Kerr, Diane Court, Jon Lewis, Norman Stockwell, Joshua Hodas, Brad Zuke, John Cronin, Jim O'Connell, Michael Haire, Susan Bricker, Dave Zobel, Peter Willcox, Bruce Holley, Don Emmons, Larry Mantrone, Frank Roosevelt, Basia Yakaitis, Robert Crooke, Judith Bonney, David Gans, Rita Hurault, Alan Thomas, Mike Stanko, Karen Zang, Ellen Jacobs, Eileen Charbonneau and Jack Simel.

Thanks also to my friend Chip Berlet and all the very good people involved with the Defending Dissent Foundation – defendingdissent.org – which was originally launched in 1960 as the National Committee to Abolish HUAC. Thankfully, the HUAC died an ignominious death in 1975, but threats to free speech and freedom to dissent continue. Thus the great need for the Defending Dissent Foundation and organizations like it.

Special thanks to Arthur Goldwag, for giving me the benefit of his invaluable criticism, to Monte Rogneby and James Malchow, for providing important research resources, and to my family, without whom nothing would be worthwhile.

ABOUT THE AUTHOR

Edward Renehan serves as Managing Director of the publishing firm New Street Communications, which includes the subsidiaries Dark Hall Press and New Street Nautical Audio. He is the author of many books including *The Secret Six* (Crown, 1995), *The Lion's Pride* (Oxford University Press, 1998), *The Kennedys at War* (Doubleday, 2002) and *Dark Genius of Wall Street* (Basic Books, 2005). His articles and reviews have appeared in such publications as the *San Francisco Chronicle*, Hearst's *Veranda* and the *Wall Street Journal*. Renehan was close friends with Toshi and Pete Seeger for more than four decades. He lives near Newport, RI.

ALSO OF INTEREST
FROM NEW STREET

*Capsized: Jim Nalepka's Epic 119 Day Survival Voyage
Aboard the Rose Noëlle*
By Steven Callahan
"Soulful, emotional ... earnest and engrossing." - KIRKUS

*Beast: A Slightly Irreverent Tale About Cancer (And Other
Assorted Anecdotes)*
By James Capuano
"A surprisingly life-affirming tale." - Susan Sarandon

Hemingway's Paris: Our Paris?
by H.R. Stoneback
"Stoneback's lyrical prose takes the reader inside the soul of
Hemingway's Paris, penetrating the surface of guide-books to
reveal tantalizing secrets." - A.E. Hotchner

Why Read Thoreau's WALDEN?
By Daniel G. Payne
"With passionate concision and eloquence, Daniel Payne urges
us to heed Thoreau's call to awaken to our lives and to the
world's sublime grandeur, and reminds us why the wisdom
found in the pages of *Walden* is more timely than ever." - Tim
Folger, Contributing Editor, DISCOVER Magazine

Made in the USA
San Bernardino, CA
19 September 2014